Darian Leader is a psychoanalyst practising in London and a
member of the Centre for Freudian Analysis and Research and
of the College of Psychoanalysts – UK. He is a Visiting Professor
at the Royal College of Art and the author of *Why do women write
more letters than they post?*, *Promises lovers make when it gets late*,
Freud's Footnotes and *Stealing the Mona Lisa* and co-author,
with David Corfield, of *Why Do People Get Ill?*

T0058010

The New Black

Mourning, Melancholia and Depression

DARIAN LEADER

Graywolf Press

The New Black: Mourning, Melancholia and Depression was first published by Hamish Hamilton, a division of Penguin Books Ltd, in 2008. This edition is published under a license from Penguin Books Ltd.

Publication of this volume is made possible in part by a grant provided by the Minnesota State Arts Board, through an appropriation by the Minnesota State Legislature; a grant from the Wells Fargo Foundation Minnesota; and a grant from the National Endowment for the Arts, which believes that a great nation deserves great art. Significant support has also been provided by the Bush Foundation; Target; the McKnight Foundation; and other generous contributions from foundations, corporations, and individuals. To these organizations and individuals we offer our heartfelt thanks.

Published by Graywolf Press
212 Third Avenue North, Suite 485
Minneapolis, Minnesota 55401
All rights reserved.

www.graywolfpress.org

Published in the United States of America

ISBN 978-1-55597-542-5

Library of Congress Control Number: 2009926854

Cover design: Kapo Ng @ A-Men Project

For Mary

Contents

Introduction

After receiving a prescription for one of the most popular anti-depressant drugs and picking them up from her chemist, a young woman returned home and opened the small packet. She had imagined a yellowish bottle filled with tightly packed capsules, like vitamin pills. Instead she found flat metallic wrapping, with each pill separated from its neighbour by a disproportionate expanse of empty foil. 'Each pill is in total solitude,' she said, 'like in metal shells looking out at each other. They are all in their individual little prisons. Why aren't they all together in one box, loose and free?' The way the pills were packaged troubled her. 'They're aligned like obedient little soldiers – why doesn't at least one of them break rank?' Her next thought was to swallow all the pills together. When I asked her why, she said, 'So they don't feel so lonely and claustrophobic.'

Although anti-depressant drugs are prescribed to millions of people in the Western world, with figures rising steadily in other countries, it seems to have occurred to no one purveying a medical cure for depression that the remedy may function as a mirror for the malady. The solitary pill sends back a cruel message to whoever opens the packet. This bleak image of separated units conveys the negative side of modern individualism, where each of us is taken to be an isolated agent, cut off from others and driven by competition for goods and services in the market-place rather than by community and shared effort.

Of course, the packaging of anti-depressants has its reasons. Isolating the pills allows the user to keep track of how many they have taken. It allows, one might say, a better management of the depression. There might even be the thought that by separating each pill with a plane of empty foil or plastic the user is discouraged from taking too many. But how many people, we might wonder, have stared at the wrapping of their anti-depressants with thoughts similar to those of the young woman above?

We could see this situation as a metaphor for the way that depression is so often treated in today's society. The interior life of the sufferer is left unexamined, and priority given to medicalizing solutions. Following the instructions for pill-taking becomes more important than examining the person's actual relation to the pills. Depression here is conceived of as a biological problem like a bacterial infection, which requires a specific biological remedy. Sufferers have to be returned to their former productive and happy states. In other words, the exploration of human interiority is being replaced with a fixed idea of mental hygiene. The problem has to be got rid of rather than understood.

Could this way of looking at depression be a part of the problem itself? As so many different aspects of the human condition are explained today in terms of biological deficits, people become emptied of the complexity of their unconscious mental life. Depression is deemed to be the result of a lack of serotonin rather than a response to experiences of loss and separation. Medication aims to restore the sufferer to the optimal levels of social adjustment and utility, with little regard for the long-term causes and possible effects of their psychological problems.

Yet the more that society sees human life in these mechanistic terms, the more that depressive states are likely to ramify. To treat a depression on the same model as, say, an infection requiring antibiotics, is always a dangerous decision. The medicine will not cure what has made the person depressed in the first place, and the more that the symptoms are seen as signs of deviance or unadapted behaviour, the more the sufferer will feel the weight of the norm, of what they are supposed to be. They become casualties of today's view of human beings as 'resources', in which a person is just a unit of energy, a packet of skills and competencies which can be bought and sold in the market-place. If that is what human life has become, is it surprising that so many people choose to refuse this fate, losing their energy and their market potential as they fall into depression and misery?

I argue in this book that we need to give up the concept of depression as it is currently framed. Instead, we should see what we call depression as a set of symptoms that derive from complex and always different human stories. These stories will involve the experiences of separation and loss, even if sometimes we are unaware of them. We are often affected by events in our lives without realizing their importance or how they have changed us. In order to make sense of how we have responded to such experiences, we need to have the right conceptual tools, and these, I think, can be found in the old notions of mourning and melancholia. Depression is a vague term for a variety of states. Mourning and melancholia, however, are more precise concepts that can help shed light on how we deal – or fail to deal – with the losses that are part of human life.

In popular psychology, mourning is often equated with the idea of getting over a loss. But do we ever get over our losses? Don't we, rather, make them a part of our lives in different ways, sometimes fruitfully, sometimes catastrophically, but never painlessly? A more careful, detailed view of mourning would explore its mechanisms and vicissitudes. As for melancholia, this is usually considered an outdated category, a topic of historical curiosity, or as a poetic term for a mood of self-absorbed sadness. As we will see, there is much more to it than that, and it can help us to understand some of the most serious cases of depression in which a person is convinced that their life is worthless and unliveable.

When I re-read Freud's brief, crisp essay *Mourning and Melancholia* a few years ago, it struck me how little had been written about mourning by later generations of analysts. There had been countless descriptions of the behaviour of people coping with loss, but much less on the deeper psychology of mourning. Freud's colleague Karl Abraham had written some brilliant papers on the subject and his own pupil Melanie Klein had made mourning central to her vision of psychical development. Yet the comments of later analysts seemed more reserved. In fact, most of the English-language literature on the themes of Freud's essay could be read in a matter of weeks. Compared to the mountain of books, papers and conference proceedings on other psychoanalytic topics that would have taken years to read through, the literature on mourning was minimal. I wondered why.

The same was true of melancholia. Apart from a few historical studies, analysts had written very little on what had certainly struck Freud as a crucial concept. What could explain this neglect? One answer seemed obvious. Where mourning and melancholia had once been received terms, today everyone talks about depression. The disappearance of the older terms could be understood in relation to the ubiquity of the newer concept. Outdated categories had been replaced by an up-to-date and more precise idea, and there has certainly been no absence of literature on depression. It is indeed such a vast field of research that it would be impossible to keep up with everything published.

Yet even a cursory glance at much of the current work on depression shows that this cannot be the solution to our question. The problems today's researchers focus on are far removed from those that preoccupied Freud and his students. Their complicated theories of how we respond mentally to the experience of loss had been replaced with descriptions of surface behaviour, dubious biochemistry and shallow psychology. Nowhere in the statistics and charts was the actual reported speech of the patients themselves, as if listening no longer mattered. The richness of the earlier research had been lost. Gone was the intricacy and concern with human subjectivity that had characterized the studies of the early analysts. It just wasn't the same set of problems. Was this progress?

Another idea then occurred to me. I had gone to a local bookshop in the hope of finding some recent studies on the theme of loss. After browsing through the non-fiction and finding nothing new, I turned to the fiction shelves. Here were books from every corner of the world, written by young novelists, seasoned favourites and the great masters of the past. So many of them were clearly stories of loss, separation and bereavement. For a moment, the sheer quantity of works dazed me. I had spent weeks puzzled by the absence of literature on my research theme, and now I was confronted with shelf after shelf of work on little else. It then occurred to me that perhaps the scientific literature on mourning that I had been searching for was simply *all literature*. This sea of books on every imaginable topic was in fact the scientific literature on mourning. And this set me thinking about the relation between mourning, loss and creativity. What place did the arts have in the process of mourning? And could the arts in fact be a vital tool in allowing us to make sense of the losses inevitable in all of our lives?

This still hardly answered my questions. What sense could we make of the categories of mourning and melancholia today? Did the old Freudian concepts still have the same purchase or did something new need to be added? How should the two concepts be differentiated and how would they allow us to re-think the terrible states of pain and anguish felt by those who complain of depression? In order to start thinking about these questions, the first step was to lift the heavy blanket off the term 'depression' itself. It is used so widely and with such little care that it acts as a barrier to exploring the detail of our responses to loss. Modern Western societies have increasingly bought into the concept of depression over the last thirty or so years, yet with little real justification. The fact that the diagnosis has achieved such dominance demands explanation.

The more that the idea of depression is used un-critically, and human responses to loss become reduced to biochemical problems, the less space there is to explore the intricate structures of mourning and melan-cholia that had so fascinated Freud. I will argue that these concepts need to be revived, and that the idea of depression should be used merely as a descriptive term to refer to surface features of behaviour. After a brief introduction to some of the debates about depression today, I turn to look at Freud's theories in detail. These have been criticized by later analysts, and we will see how both Karl Abraham and Melanie Klein made important contributions to the study of loss in the wake of Freud's initial research. Although their ideas may today seem far-fetched or at best outdated, we will see how there is still much to learn from them.

After the early groundbreaking work, one crucial criticism of Freud's essay became unavoidable. Freud saw mourning as an individual task, yet every documented human society gives a central place to public mourning rituals. Loss would be inscribed within the community through a system of rites, customs and codes, ranging from changes in dress and eating habits to highly stylized memorial ceremonies. These involved not just the bereaved individual and their immediate family, but the much larger social group. Yet why would loss have to be dealt with publicly? And if today's societies, suspicious of such public displays, tend to make grief more and more a private event, the domain of the individual, could this have an effect on mourning itself? Is mourning more difficult today because of this erosion of social mourning rites? Mourning, I will argue, requires other people.

Exploring these questions brings us to define the tasks of mourning. Grief may be our first reaction to loss, but grief and mourning are not exactly the same thing. If we lose someone we love, be it through death or separation, mourning is never an automatic process. For many people, in fact, it never happens. We will describe four aspects of the mourning process that signal that the work of thinking through loss is taking place. Without these we may remain caught in a stagnant, unresolved mourning or a melancholia. In mourning, we grieve the dead; in melancholia, we die with them. In the last section, we sketch a theory of melancholia that builds on Freud's ideas and offers an account of the key place of creativity in this painful and ravaging condition.

—

I would like to thank several people for their contributions to this book. First of all, my analysands, for their insights, effort and courage to speak about what is most painful in their lives. So much of what follows has been formulated by them and I have often felt that I was doing little more than transcribing their words. I also owe a great deal to Geneviève Morel, whose work has provided continual inspiration for my exploration of mourning and melancholia. A study group at the Centre for Freudian Analysis and Research allowed me to elaborate many of the themes of the book, and I would like to thank CFAR for all its support. Special thanks also to Ed Cohen, whose interest, encouragement and critique were invaluable, and to the friends and colleagues who have contributed to the book: Maria Alvarez, Pat Blackett, Vincent Dachy, Marie Darrieussecq, Abi Fellows, Astrid Gessert, Anouchka Grose, Franz Kaltenbeck, Michael Kennedy, Hanif Kureishi, Janet Low, Zoe Manzi, Pete Owen, Vicken Parsons, Hara Pepeli, Alan Rowan and Lindsay Watson. Dany Nobus was kind enough to publish a first technical draft of some of my research in the *Journal for Lacanian Studies*. At Hamish Hamilton, Simon Prosser was a perfect editor, Anna Ridley and Francesca Main provided much-needed help, and Georgina Capel at Capel-Land was as ever a gracious and patient agent.

I

Depression today is everywhere. GPs diagnose it, celebrities reveal they suffer from it, children are given prescriptions for it, media articles debate it, soap opera characters wrestle with it. Yet forty years ago depression was hardly anywhere. A tiny percentage of the population were deemed to suffer depression, and it had little dignity as a diagnostic category. People were *anxious* or *neurotic*, but not depressed. This is sometimes explained in terms of a growth in scientific knowledge. Since it is only today that we really understand what depression is, we can look back and realize how it had always been present yet undiagnosed. The burgeoning of the diagnosis is simply a sign of scientific progress.

From this perspective, depression is the name of a unique disease. It has specific biological markers and is found in all human societies. It involves symptoms such as insomnia, poor appetite and low energy, and this loss of biological, vital tone is ascribed to a chemical problem in the brain. Once we have developed these initial symptoms, culture may then help to shape them, giving prominence to some and encouraging us to remain discreet about others. We might have no problem telling our friends or our doctor about feeling exhausted, but remain reserved about revealing our loss of libido.

According to this view, our biological states will

become interpreted as moods and emotions by our cultural surroundings. Low energy, for example, may become interpreted as 'sadness' or 'guilt' in one society but not in another. Similarly, how a culture responds to these feelings will vary widely, ranging from concern and care to disregard and dismissal. Some cultures will supply rich vocabularies to describe these feelings and will accord legitimacy to them, while others will not. On this view, what we call 'depression' is the particular Western medical interpretation of a certain set of biological states, with brain chemistry the basic problem.

An alternative perspective sees depression as the result of profound changes in our societies. The rise of market-driven economies creates a breakdown of social support mechanisms and of the sense of community. People lose their feeling of being connected to social groups and so feel depleted and solitary. Deprived of resources, economically unstable, subject to acute pressures and with few alternative pathways and hopes, they fall ill. The causes of depression, according to this view, are social. Sustained social pressures are bound to end up affecting our bodies, but the pressures come first, the biological responses second.

This social view is echoed in the perspective of some psychoanalysts, who see depression as a form of protest. As humans are taken to be units of energy in industrialized societies, they will resist, whether they are conscious of this or not. Thus, much of what is today labelled depression could be understood as old-fashioned hysteria, in the sense of a refusal of current forms of mastery and domination. The more that society insists on the values of efficiency and economic productivity, the more depression will proliferate as a necessary consequence. In a similar way, the more modern society urges us to attain autonomy and independence in our search for fulfilment, the more resistance will take the form of the exact opposite of these values. It puts misery in the midst of plenty. Depression is thus a way of saying NO to what we are told to be.

—

According to the World Health Organization, by 2010 depression will be the single largest public health problem after heart disease. It will affect between 25 and 45 per cent of the adult population, with rising rates in children and adolescents. According to the American Academy of Child and Adolescent Psychiatry, there are currently nearly 3.5 million depressed children in the US, and more than 6 per cent of American children are taking psychiatric medication. Back in 1950, however, depression was estimated to affect only 0.5 per cent of the population. What could have happened over the last half century?

Historians of psychiatry and psychoanalysis have mostly agreed that depression was created as a clinical category by a variety of factors in the second half of the twentieth century: there was a pressure to package psychological problems like other health problems, and so a new emphasis on surface behaviour rather than on unconscious mechanisms came to the fore; the market for minor tranquillizers collapsed in the 1970s after their addictive properties were publicized and so a new diagnostic category – and remedy for it – had to be popularized to account for and cater to the malaise of urban populations; and new laws about drug-testing favoured a simplistic, discrete conception of what illness was. As a result, drugs companies manufactured both the idea of the illness and the cure at the same time. Most of the published research had been funded by them, and depression came to stand less for a complex of symptoms with varied unconscious causes than simply that which anti-depressants acted on. If the drugs affected mood, appetite and sleep patterns, then depression consisted of a problem with mood, appetite and sleep patterns. Depression, in other words, was created as much as it was discovered.

Today, there is some scepticism about the claims made for anti-depressant drugs. It is now well known that most studies of their effectiveness are industry-funded and that, until very recently, negative results were hardly ever published. Claims for the specificity of the drugs have also been seriously put in question. But, despite such wariness, the idea of depression as a brain problem retains its attraction even for the sceptics. When newspaper articles point to the dangers of particular drugs like Seroxat, suggesting that they increase the risk of suicide, the reasons for this are then explained biochemically: the drug causes the suicidal thoughts. These critics of the drug thus share the belief of its makers: that our thoughts and actions can be determined biochemically.

The implication of such critiques is simply that the drugs aren't good enough: they need to be more specific, promoting positive rather than negative thoughts. This perspective ignores completely the idea that the suicides may sometimes be due to poor initial diagnosis – for example, as we will see later on, mis-diagnosing melancholia as 'depression' – and, just as significantly, failing to consider that depression may itself be a protective mechanism which, if removed, makes desperate action more likely. Some studies, in fact, have claimed that mild depressions may actually protect *against* suicide. In other cases, the way that the drug dumbs down a person's mental states may short-circuit the production of genuine defences against suicidal feelings.

The myth of depression as an exclusively biological disease has come to replace the detailed study of the variety of human responses to loss and disappointment. Social and economic forces have certainly played their part here in this effort to transform grief into depression. We are taught to see nearly every aspect of the human condition as in some sense subject to our conscious choice and potential control, and so when drugs companies market their products they play on these modern ingredients of our self-image. We might be ill, but we can choose to take the drugs and so become well. Not to do so would appear irrational and self-destructive. Even in the shanty towns of Lima in Peru, large colourful posters urge the public to ask their GPs for name-brand anti-depressants. The drugs, it is claimed, will restore us to our former selves.

Although plenty of studies exist which show that anti-depressants, in fact, do not do what they are supposed to do, our society seems only to have ears for the positive PR. We know that most research is industry-funded, that the drugs are not as specific as they claim to be, that they do have serious side-effects and produce significant withdrawal problems and that, over time, psychotherapy provides a better and more solid treatment. Yet the prescriptions still continue, together with new and scientific-sounding propaganda issuing from the drugs companies. Worldwide, this constitutes a market that runs into billions of dollars, and it would be difficult to imagine anyone within the industry deciding that the time was right to close it down.

In Britain, the drugs industry is the third most profitable economic activity, after tourism and finance. The NHS spends around £7 billion on medications in England, with around 80 per cent of that spent on patented brand products. This might seem to necessitate non-partisan evaluation of research, yet today 27 of the 35 members of the Government committee charged with selecting and approving drugs for the NHS receive private salaries from the pharmaceuticals industry. Where an individual researcher studying such drugs may get journal offprints of 50 or 100 copies of their work to send to colleagues, industry-funded results may run to 100,000 reprints and then benefit from free distribution to doctors. These economic factors create the illusion that there is a balance of opinion in favour of the drugs.

The problem here is not just about access to information but what counts as information in the first place. Studying a particular anti-depressant may not prove so difficult, but a project which sets out to question the very validity of anti-depressants themselves will not find funding easily. To conduct such studies and disseminate their results requires powerful backing, which means the kind of money that only industry really has. In addition, for such studies to count as 'scientific' they must use the same language and diagnostic systems as the purveyors of the drugs. Otherwise, no meaningful comparisons, it is believed, can be made. This has the unfortunate result that even the most basic concepts – such as depression itself – tend to avoid critical scrutiny.

Yet why should we see depression as a single, unique entity? Clearly, this is what the drugs industry wants us to do, since this is what allows the sale of drugs that claim to treat it. But we should not hold the pharmaceuticals companies solely responsible here. Contemporary society – which means us – also plays its part in shaping how we wish to see ourselves and our ailments. When things go wrong, we want to be able to name the problem quickly, which makes us all the more receptive to the labels that doctors and drugs companies offer us. Most of us also want to avoid the labour of exploring our inner lives, which means that we prefer to see symptoms as signs of some local disturbance rather than difficulties which concern our whole existence. Being able to group our feelings of malaise, anxiety or sadness under the blanket term 'depression' and then take a pill for it will naturally seem more attractive than putting our whole life under a psychological microscope.

But what if depression itself were as multiple and varied as those who are told that they suffer from it?

Why not see the manifest symptoms of depression as more akin to states like fever: they might look the same across a wide range of people but their causes will be quite diverse. Just as a fever may be a sign of malaria or of a common flu virus, so loss of appetite, say, could be a sign of being in love without knowing it or of a refusal of the overwhelming demands of other people or of some private grief. Discovering these causes can never be achieved in the space of a ten- or twenty-minute GP consultation, but requires long and detailed listening and dialogue. There is a crucial difference between surface phenomena, such as apathy, insomnia and loss of appetite, and the underlying problems which are generating these states, usually far removed from our conscious awareness.

What about the psychological therapies here? Surely they are available through GPs and hospitals and provide the necessary counterpoint to drug-based treatments? Don't they provide precisely the space for listening that the depressed patient needs? Unfortunately this is far from the case. Psychological therapies are often available, but the term itself can be misleading: it nearly always means short-term cognitive behavioural therapy (CBT) and hardly ever refers to long-term psychoanalytic psychotherapy. CBT sees people's symptoms as the outcome of faulty learning. With proper re-education, they can correct their behaviour and bring it closer to the desired norm. In itself, CBT is a form of conditioning that aims at mental hygiene. It has no place for the realities of sexuality or violence that lie at the heart of human life. These are seen as anomalies or learning errors rather than as primary and fundamental drives. Symptoms, likewise, are not seen as the bearers of truth but rather as mistakes to be avoided, an issue we will return to later on in this book.

CBT, however, is almost the only psychological therapy on offer through healthcare trusts. This is for a very simple reason: it works. But not in the sense we might wish for. As a superficial treatment, it cannot access unconscious complexes and drives. What it can do is provide results on paper that keep NHS managers happy. It comes equipped with its own evaluative tests and questionnaires, which tend to give very positive results. On paper, it can help get rid of symptoms and make people happier. But aside from the fact that questionnaire methods are notoriously unreliable, it takes no account of the future or alternative symptoms people may develop later on. When these appear, the patient ends up back on a waiting list, and since the surface symptom may well be different now, it won't look as if the first treatment failed. Once again, the difference between surface phenomena and underlying structure is ignored.

Psychoanalytic approaches to depression are very different from those of CBT. If a patient says, 'I'm depressed', the analyst will not claim to know what this means or what would be best for them. On the contrary, it will be a question of unpacking what the words mean for that particular individual and exploring how their present problems have been shaped by their unconscious mental life. The analyst does not know better than the patient here and their primary goal is not the removal of symptoms, even if this turns out to be a result. Rather, what matters is to allow what is being expressed in the symptom to be articulated, however at odds with social norms this might be. The patient is the expert here and not the analyst.

The patient certainly knows more than the analyst about the sources of his or her problems, but this knowledge is rather peculiar. It is not conscious but unconscious knowledge. The patient knows it without knowing it, in the same way that we can be aware that our dreams mean something without being able to explain or interpret them. Analysis will aim to bring unconscious material to light, and this will always be a difficult and unpredictable process. Nothing can be known in advance, and the relationship between patient and analyst may well turn out to be as turbulent as any other form of intimate human bond. These features of analysis mean that it can hardly fit in with what our contemporary anti-risk society deems desirable: swift and predictable results, absolute transparency and the removal of unwanted behaviour. It is precisely CBT and not analysis that claims to offer these latter solutions. The price to be paid, however, is a cosmetic treatment that targets surface problems and not deep underlying ones.

Thinking about mourning and melancholia allows us to move beyond these surface features to what lies beneath them. Unlike publicizing the latest anti-depressant drug, it does not mean big business for anyone. Yet as we read through paper after paper on depression considered as a brain disease, we totally lose any sense that at the core of many people's experience of inertia and lack of interest in life lies the loss of a cherished human relationship or a crisis of personal meaning. If these factors are recognized at all, they become transformed into vague talk of 'stress' and relegated to the diagnostic periphery. In our new dark ages, individual experience and unconscious interior life no longer have any place in the way we are encouraged to think about ourselves. Our wants and wishes are taken at face value, rather than seen as masking conflicts and often incompatible unconscious desires.

Depression is far too general a term to help us here. Although not all occurrences of depressive states indicate an underlying mourning or melancholia, these concepts can none the less allow us to approach the problem of loss with greater clarity. They can tell us something about why a depressive reaction can develop into a serious, sustained dejection or, at times, into a terrible, unending nightmare of self-accusation and guilt. In everyday life, the most obvious triggers for depressive states concern our self-image. Something happens to make us question the way we would like to be seen: our boss makes a critical comment, our lover becomes more distant, our colleagues fail to acknowledge some achievement. In other words, an ideal image of ourselves as lovable is punctured.

But depressions are just as likely not only when an ideal image is compromised but when we actually manage to attain our ideal: the athlete who breaks a world record, the seducer who finally makes his conquest, the worker who gets the long-awaited promotion. In these instances, our desire is suddenly removed. We might have striven for years to achieve some goal, but when there is no longer anything to attain we feel the presence of a void at the core of our lives. Most people will have experienced this in some form after finishing exams. The long-awaited moment has been reached, and now there is only the blues.

These depressive states do not always lead to long, serious periods of despair and despondency, but, when they do, we can suspect that questions of mourning and, in some cases, of melancholia are at play. Ups and downs are of course a part of human life, and it would be a mistake to pathologize every episode of the blues. But when the downs start to snowball, gathering their own depressive momentum, we must ask what other problems they have revived or absorbed. In most cases, these will not be available to conscious introspection, and will require careful analysis and dialogue to become clearer.

A young woman fell into a profound depression when she was finally able to move in with her boyfriend. They had continued a long-distance relationship for two years, travelling on alternate weekends across the Atlantic to see each other. When he agreed to relocate to London, it seemed as if the gruelling schedule of flights, jet-lag and exhaustion would at last end. Now they could be together and share a space for the first time. Both were filled with hope, yet no more than a few days after his arrival, she became sad, inert and anxious. As these feelings became more pervasive, the relationship collapsed, and it was only years later in her analysis that she was able to make sense of what had precipitated her depressive state. Why had it all fallen apart precisely at the moment she had what she wanted?

The immediate explanation was simply that she now no longer had a desire. The relationship had been characterized by longing and distance, and now that these barriers were removed, there was nothing left to yearn for. The depression was a consequence of the void that this attainment had introduced. Although there may well be some truth in this view, the situation was in fact more complex. What, after all, had the long-distance relationship consisted of? As she described the weekend trips to and from the States, she realized that the key for her had been the moments of departure; the moments, in other words, when she had to say goodbye. Her memories were focused around these tearful and emotional scenes at Heathrow or JFK. But why would they have mattered so much?

When she was fourteen, her father had died of cancer, yet no one in the family had told her either what he was suffering from or that it would prove fatal. She knew that he was unwell, yet the news of his death came as a dreadful and unpredicted shock. She had assumed all along that she would see him soon, yet when she was led out of the classroom at school to receive the bad news, it was as if, she said, 'nothing made sense any more'. He had been in hospital for several weeks, yet she had not been able to see him. He died without her ever having been able to say goodbye.

She now understood what had kept her relationship with her boyfriend going and also what had ended it. It was no accident that she had fallen in love with a man who lived so far away. The weekend trips allowed her to stage what she called 'one hundred goodbyes'.

Each time they parted, she would say goodbye passionately, exactly as she had never been able to do with her father. It was at the precise moment that she could no longer say goodbye – when the boyfriend had moved to London and thus removed the distance between them – that her love began to wane and the depression started. Beneath the depressive feelings was an unresolved mourning for her dead father.

—

To start thinking about the question of loss and mourning, we can begin with Freud's brief essay *Mourning and Melancholia*, drafted in 1915 and published some two years later. We might take it for granted that both mourning and melancholia involve responses to a loss, yet when Freud wrote his essay this was far from obvious. If mourning refers to the work of grief subsequent to a loss, associating melancholia with the experience of loss was by no means a received viewpoint. Before Freud, the medical literature had not linked them in such a systematic way.

Reading earlier texts, we come across occasional associations between melancholia and loss, but these tend to be treated as contingent and rather episodic details. Robert Burton, author of the vast *Anatomy of Melancholy*, first published in 1621, quipped that melancholy was 'known to few, unknown to fewer', but recent studies of the concept of melancholy have highlighted its shifting forms and the instability of its characterizing symptoms. If we associate it today with the blues or a painful nostalgia, it was often linked in the past to manic states or to periods of creativity.

Looking through the different descriptions, the most common symptoms would be a sense of fear and sorrow without obvious cause. Until well into the nineteenth century, sadness and feeling low were not defining features of melancholy. Indeed, fixation on a single theme, later known as monomania, was a much more common criterion. And the clinical picture of melancholia that we can distil from such accounts puts a greater emphasis on anxiety than on depressive feelings.

This might seem surprising, especially given the tendency of some psychiatric thinking to separate anxiety from depression. Although most working psychiatrists are well aware that the two states cannot be so readily differentiated, it is still common in the literature to find the two treated separately. Yet anyone who has experienced a loss might be familiar with the unsettling rhythm of a sense of depletion followed by one of expectant dread. 'No one ever told me that grief felt so much like fear' reads the very first sentence of *A Grief Observed*, C. S. Lewis's account of his feelings after his wife's death from cancer. Anxiety, indeed, in its purest form is found in melancholia, and we will try to explain why this is the case later on.

Freud saw both mourning and melancholia as ways that human beings respond to the experience of loss, but how does he differentiate them? Mourning involves the long and painful work of detaching ourselves from the loved one we have lost. 'Its function,' Freud writes, 'is to detach the survivors' memories and hopes from the dead.' Mourning, then, is different from grief. Grief is our reaction to a loss, but mourning is how we process this grief. Each memory and expectation linked to the person we have lost must be revived and met with the judgement that they are gone for ever. This is the difficult and terrible time when our thoughts perpetually return to the one we have lost. We think of their presence in our lives, we turn over memories of moments spent together, we imagine that we see them in the street, we expect to hear their voice when the phone rings. Indeed, researchers claim that at least 50 per cent of bereaved people actually experience some form of hallucination of their lost loved one. They are there haunting us during the mourning process, but each time we think of them, some of the intensity of our feelings is being fractioned away.

Everyday actions like going to the shops, walking in a park, going to the cinema or being in certain parts of one's city suddenly become incredibly painful. Each place we visit, even the most familiar, revives memories of when we were there with the person we loved. If shopping at the supermarket or walking down the street with one's partner had never been a particularly special experience, doing it now becomes painful. It isn't just the revival of happy memories linked to those places that matters, but the fact of knowing that we won't see them there ever again. Even new experiences can become agonizing. Seeing a film, viewing an exhibition or listening to a piece of music make us want to share it with the one we've lost. The fact that they aren't there makes our everyday reality seem acutely lacking. The world around us seems to harbour an empty space, a void. It loses its magic.

Over time our attachment will lessen. Freud told one of his patients that this process would take between one and two years. But it would not be easy. We recoil, he said, from any activity that causes pain, and so there is 'a revolt in our minds against mourning'. This is an important and perhaps neglected point. Freud is suggesting that there might be nothing natural about mourning. It won't happen automatically, and we might even be doing our best to resist it without being aware of this consciously. If, however, we are able to follow the mourning process through, the pain will grow less, together with our feelings of remorse and self-reproach. We realize little by little that the one we've loved is gone, and the energy of our attachment to them will become gradually loosened so that one day it may become linked to someone else. We will realize that life still has something to offer.

A woman who had lost her mother at a very young age was haunted by the powerful image of the sweet-shop where she had worked. The details of the shop, the colours and odours were all as present to her as they had been so many years ago, and, as she observed, they were now even more so. The mother's death had made these sensations sharper, as if they had been amplified by her absence. As they took on the value of a marker for the lost mother, so they grew in intensity. Yet after a protracted and difficult work of mourning, the sweet-shop appeared to her in a dream surrounded, for the first time, by other shops. 'The sweet-shop,' she said, 'was just one shop among all the others.' The mourning had loosened the attachment to the one privileged marker, and the shop was no longer special.

Freud doesn't refer simply to mourning here. He uses the expression 'the work of mourning', in a phrase that echoes the concept he had already introduced in his book *The Interpretation of Dreams*, 'the dream work' or 'the work of dreaming'. The dream work is what transforms a thought or wish we might have into the manifest, complex dream. It consists of displacements, distortions and condensations, equivalent to the mechanisms of the unconscious itself. Freud uses the same kind of expression to talk about mourning to indicate, perhaps, that it isn't just our thoughts about the lost loved one that count, but what we do with them: how they are organized, arranged, run through, altered. In this process, our memories and hopes about the one we've lost must be brought up in all the different ways they have been registered, like looking at a diamond not just from one angle but from all possible angles, so that each of its facets can be viewed. In Freudian terms, the lost object must be accessed in all its varying representations.

When Freud talks about the lost object here he doesn't just mean a person lost through death. The phrase can also refer to a loss that is brought about through separation or estrangement. The one we've lost may still be there in reality, although the nature of our link to them will have changed. They might even be living in the same house, or the same city, and it is clear that the meaning of loss will depend on the particular circumstances of each individual. Bereavement is perhaps the clearest example of a loss since it marks a real, empirical absence, but Freud intended his ideas to have a much wider scope. What matters will be the removal of any reference point that has been important in our lives and that has become the focus of our attachments. In mourning, this reference point is not just removed, but its absence is registered, inscribed indelibly in our mental lives.

—

It is tempting to associate Freud's idea of the work of mourning with some of the developments in art taking place around the same time that he wrote his essay. There, in the Cubism of Picasso and Braque, we see the image of a human being reassembled as a group of multiple perspectives. Different angles and aspects of the conventional image of a person or object are combined and reshuffled to give the resulting Cubist image. The model becomes equivalent to a series of fragments seen from different points, a process that seems to embody Freud's notion of a person being mourned through the piecemeal collection of our representations of them.

This parallel between the artistic process and the work of mourning can be found in other practices beyond Cubism. Think, for example, of the very different art of de Chirico and Morandi. In de Chirico's work, we see the same collection of motifs – a fountain, a shadow, a train on the horizon – repeated again and again but in different configurations. The elements are often identical, but their arrangement changes. These paintings occupied him for at least fifty years, and were sometimes produced on a daily basis. In Morandi's work, we see the same group of bottles and jugs moved around endlessly to create different configurations. Their composition even evokes comparison with a family portrait, as if the jugs and tableware had taken the place of family members arranged carefully to be photographed. Like the work of mourning described by Freud, a set of representations is given a special value, focused on and reshuffled.

Mourning for Freud involves the movement of reshuffling and rearranging. We think of our lost loved one time and time again, in different situations, different poses, different moods, different places and different contexts. As the writer and psychiatrist Gordon Livingstone observed, after losing his six-year-old son to leukaemia, 'Perhaps that's how it is with a permanent loss: you examine it from every angle you can think of and then just carry it like a weight.' If this aspect of the work of mourning will eventually exhaust itself, why is it that Morandi or de Chirico remained caught for so long reconfiguring the same elements? It was quite common in the art of the nineteenth century to produce multiple variants of the same image, understood as a quest for perfection, but there is something more here than the practice of an old artistic vogue. Pursuing the analogy with mourning, might this indicate an arrest or stagnation of the mourning process?

We tend to repeat things when we remain trapped in them. When Edgar Allan Poe's mother died when he was a boy of almost three, he was left alone in the house overnight with his baby sister and the corpse until a family benefactor found them. In his work he returns again and again to the image of the blank stare of the dead, and the proximity of death is everywhere. Burials are premature, bodies won't stay dead, dying chambers stretch out to infinity, cadavers rot and decay, and blood seeps from a corpse's mouth. Before his own death, the spectre of a ghostly woman that haunts these stories would invade his waking life in a series of terrifying hallucinations. Poe's literary effort to describe this encounter with death from every possible angle suggests that the work of mourning could not be completed. Rather than laying his mother to rest, her presence became increasingly real, despite his attempt to transpose the horror of what had happened to another, symbolic level through his writing.

Trying to represent an experience from several different angles is an essential part of the work of mourning, but other processes are also necessary, as we shall see. Before turning to this question, it is worth exploring the notion of multiple views a bit further with an example taken from the work of contemporary artist Susan Hiller. In her recent 'J-Street Project', she presents a visual catalogue of all the streetnames containing the word 'Jew' that had been restored after their removal during Nazi Germany. We see images of 'Jew Street', 'Jew Alley', 'Jew Gardens', one after the other. Isn't there something evocative here of the work of mourning described by Freud – the piecemeal, serial movement through different representations of the same thing: a streetsign with the word 'Jew' in it?

But Hiller's work is less about mourning than about what can go wrong with it. If we see Morandi's and de Chirico's relentless rearrangement of the same elements as examples of a stagnant, blocked mourning, perhaps 'J-Street Project' can be understood as a commentary on this very impediment. It becomes increasingly difficult for us to invent stories around the signs, in the way that we might when we lose ourselves in an enigmatic, beautiful painting. Rather than the in-depth exploration of a single street, the characters that once inhabited it, their lives, hopes and dreams, there is simply a visual list. Instead of a story, there is a sequence. Perhaps this reflects the fact that there is a basic problem of mourning here. Every attempt to give the Holocaust a narrative frame risks turning it into a story of heroism and valour or of death and defeat. This is because human narratives follow certain set patterns. Stories are always the same, as many of the philologists of the early twentieth century found out when they began to catalogue the elements of myth, folklore and fiction across different cultures. And that is precisely what makes a single story inappropriate for representing anything to do with the Holocaust.

Films such as *Schindler's List* fail so conspicuously to deal with their subject matter for exactly this reason. The moment that the conventions of the Hollywood movie are introduced, all specificity is lost and the stock narratives of the conflict between good and evil prevail. The Holocaust becomes just like any other disaster movie plot, with the same twists, turns and inevitabilities. If we agreed that the Holocaust was not reducible to one single story, how else could anything be said about it other than through lists? This is exactly what we see with a film like Claude Lanzmann's *Shoah*. Many people criticized it for just being a series of interviews, one after the other. But, as Susan Hiller's work shows, isn't this perhaps the only option available? This is in perfect contrast to Hiller's earlier work *Clinic*, in which 200 people invent stories about death. Death is like an unrepresentable point that the narratives circle around. The serial, list-like quality of 'J-Street', on the contrary, frustrates our desire to create stories, and we can find other examples of this in contemporary art. We could think, for example, of the list published by Michael Landy of the thousands of objects he destroyed in his work 'Breakdown', in which all of his personal possessions were ground into dust by a machine he had installed to literally break down his life.

The signs catalogued in 'The J-Street Project' offer a further ambiguity. They have been restituted exactly as before. Beyond the well-intentioned effort to commemorate, the message here is in fact precisely the opposite. It's as if nothing had happened in between. We are not seeing empty signs or the places where signs once hung on walls, but reality as if nothing had ever touched it: as if 'Jew Street' before and 'Jew Street' after the Holocaust were one and the same. The sign here is identical to its own forgetting. This is reinforced by the people we see in the film. They stroll by without once noticing the signs. They carry on regardless. By focusing on what are intended as memorials, Hiller has made a film about people not noticing the past. And this failure to mourn is echoed in the serial, piecemeal presentation of the images.

The work of these artists thus suggests that it isn't

just listing or reshuffling or recombining elements that constitutes mourning. Something more has to take place. On its own, the work of listing and reshuffling may indicate precisely a block to the mourning process. When Michael Landy made the list of the thousands of objects he had lost in 'Breakdown', couldn't we guess that in fact he was trying to register the loss of only one, specific thing?

—

What about melancholia? How is it distinguished from mourning? Freud argues that while the mourner knows more or less what has been lost, this is not always obvious to the melancholic. The nature of the loss is not necessarily known consciously, and may just as well involve a disappointment or slight from someone else as the loss occasioned by bereavement, or even the collapse of a political or religious ideal. If the melancholic does have an idea of whom he has lost, he does not know, Freud says, 'what he has lost' in them. This brilliant point complicates the simple picture of grief. We have to distinguish *whom we have lost* from *what we have lost in them*. And, as we will see, perhaps the difficulty of making this separation is one of the things that can block the mourning process.

The key feature of melancholia for Freud is a lowering of self-regard. Although melancholia shares with mourning such features as 'a profoundly painful dejection, cessation of interest in the outside world, loss of the capacity to love' and an inhibition of activity, its prime distinguishing trait is 'a lowering of self-regarding feelings to a degree that finds utterance in self-reproaches and self-revilings, and culminates in a delusional expectation of punishment'. The melancholic represents himself as 'poor, worthless and despicable, and expects to be cast out and punished'. Melancholia means that after a loss, one's image of oneself is profoundly altered.

The melancholic believes himself worthless and unworthy. And he will insist on this quite vocally. These comments already help to divide up the clinical picture. Many depressed people feel worthless, but the melancholic is different in that he may articulate this without the reticence often found in others. Similarly, many neurotic people will link their feelings of unworthiness or uselessness to aspects of their physical image: their body just isn't right, their nose or hair is all wrong. But the melancholic has a much deeper complaint. For him, it is the very core of his being which is unworthy or wrong, and not only its surface features. Where a neurotic might become uneasy on having an evil thought or impulse, the melancholic will condemn himself as an evil *person*. This is an onto-logical complaint, concerning his actual existence. Where the neurotic person may feel inferior to others and inadequate, the melancholic will actually accuse himself of worthlessness, as if his life itself were some kind of sin or crime. He doesn't just *feel* inadequate: he *knows* he is inadequate. There is certainty here rather than doubt.

Melancholics will berate themselves endlessly for their faults. No amount of rational advice or persuasion can stop them. They have a conviction that they are in the wrong. In contrast to the paranoiac, who blames the outside world, the melancholic only blames himself. Freud uses this motif of self-reproach as a defining feature of melancholia, thereby setting it aside from many other cases of depressive feeling. Historically, the distinction between a natural and an unnatural melancholia had often been unclear: to what extent was a certain melancholia a part of human existence and to what extent was it an illness that needed to be treated? How could one distinguish between melancholic despair and that induced by a 'true' sense of sin?

The need of the melancholic to berate himself puzzled Freud. Why this insistence on self-blame? Could it be that when the melancholic was so busy blaming himself, he was really blaming someone else? In his *Characters* of 1659, the essayist Samuel Butler claimed that 'A melancholic man is one that keeps the worst company in the world, that is, his own.' Freud has exactly the opposite thesis: that the company kept by the melancholic is that of his object. He has turned his reproaches towards someone else against himself.

These clamorous self-reproaches are in fact reproaches directed to another person who has been internalized. The melancholic has identified completely with the one they've lost. This does not always mean that a real separation or bereavement has taken place. It may be someone the person loves, or has loved or even should have loved. But once the loss has occurred, their image has been transferred into the place of the melancholic's ego. The anger and hatred directed at the lost person are similarly displaced, so that the ego is now judged as if it were the forsaken object. In

Freud's famous phrase, 'the shadow of the object' has fallen on the ego, now subject to the merciless criticism so singular to the melancholic subject. Spears have become boomerangs.

—

Let's illustrate the contrast between a neurotic self-reproach and a melancholic one. A woman presents with two symptoms: a paralysing mutism, which emerges in certain social situations, and a pervasive hypochondria, which sends her from one doctor to another. Although she has not connected the two phenomena, a relation between them certainly existed. The mutism expressed for her the proposition 'I've got nothing to say', while the hypochondriacal anxieties took the form of the belief 'I've got something inside me.' She exhausted herself with a perpetual self-reproach that there was 'something wrong' with her, that she 'wasn't right', phrases that echoed her father's continued invectives against her in her childhood and adolescence. These reproaches now took the form of her presenting symptoms.

Although the two propositions 'I've got nothing to say' and 'I've got something inside me' seemed the two opposing poles of the spectrum of her misery, her daydreams revealed a particular proximity between them. The visits to the medical specialists would from time to time result in minor operations. She would imagine how the doctors would remove something from her body, leaving, as she put it, 'nothing inside me'. The daydreams would then continue as follows: returning home to her husband, would she still be loved by him despite her loss? These scenarios evoked for her the fascination in her childhood with a certain fictional character with a missing limb. Her symptoms asked the question: 'Can I be loved with nothing inside?' And we can note that the hypochondriacal symptoms had been established in the months following her first pregnancy which ended with an abortion.

We can see how the self-reproach here, which might seem at times existential, has been linked systematically to the representation of the body. This contrasts with the clinical picture of a melancholia, where the question of bodily organs does not function in the same causal sense. Madame N———, a patient of the French psychiatrist Jules Séglas, observed that she didn't have a stomach or kidneys, but this was not the *reason* for her torments. She saw herself as the cause of all the world's evils, including her child's death from meningitis. We could contrast our patient's *question* 'Can I be loved with nothing inside?' to Mme N———'s *conclusion* 'I've got nothing inside because I didn't love.'

Neurotic symptoms are ways of asking a question. In our example, self-reproaches concealed a question about love. In a melancholia, on the contrary, the self-reproaches are less a way of asking a question than a kind of solution. The subject is guilty. They have been condemned. There is a certainty here of being the worst, the least lovable, the greatest sinner. This emphasis on the person's exceptional status (the most ..., the greatest ..., the worst ...) led Karl Abraham to caution against confusing the diagnosis of melancholia with that of paranoia. Couldn't being the worst actually be a form of megalomania?

—

For Freud, the melancholic's self-reproach is in fact a reproach to the lost loved one. But why a reproach in the first place? Surely the dead and departed only merit our sympathy? There may be anger for the very simple reason that, when someone vanishes, we hold their departure against them. Funeral chants in many cultures often bitterly chastise the deceased for having abandoned the living. And this rage is ubiquitous in the mental life of bereaved people. They may find it difficult to mourn a loss when tender feelings jostle with fury at that person for having died. Absence is never accepted without rage. Mourning a loved one, a man described his terrifying dream of a cracked gravestone, as if 'shattered by an act of revenge'. Making sense of this was difficult since he felt no conscious anger, yet further dreams showed how real this was. He couldn't forgive the dead person for departing. The dream is exemplary in that it shows how difficult it can be to build a memorial for someone if rage continually shatters it.

Trips to visit the loved one's grave brought out the same dilemma. Each time he set off for the cemetery, he would find himself in the wrong place: he would miss the correct tube stop or become lost in the maze of streets surrounding the graveyard. These misadventures left him in utter despair, until he suddenly realized that they were playing out his reproach to the dead. Finding himself alone and without bearings in a strange place, he said, it was as if he admonished the dead: 'Look what you are doing to me, you have left me lost! I've been abandoned by my guide.' This cycle of losing his way was a concealed form of fury: 'I held him responsible', he said, 'for my being left, bewildered and frightened.'

This is one of the most important discoveries of psychoanalysis: the fact that we can feel fury without being consciously aware of it. It can even emerge when we are quite literally not conscious. Several studies of behaviour during sleep have shown how acts of violence can be carried out towards the bedfellow, with absolutely no recollection upon waking. Sleep medicine experts claim that such violence, which can range from serious assault to slaps and punches, affects around 2 per cent of the general population, yet the figure is no doubt higher, given the obvious barriers against reporting it. Where the sleep medicine researchers look to brain chemistry for explanations, psychoanalysts make the hypothesis of unconscious hostility which we do our best to ignore in our waking lives and which uses night-time as its alibi.

The fact that affection and hatred are so closely linked in our emotional life is still, more than a hundred years after the invention of psychoanalysis, difficult for most people to accept. When I wrote a newspaper column about it a few years ago, an editor phoned me in bewilderment: 'How,' he asked, 'can someone feel both positive and negative feelings towards the same person?' This difficulty is no doubt one of the reasons why we tend to avoid thinking about it. Anthropologists, for example, once debated with some passion the strange ambivalence found in funeral rituals in many cultures. The dead would be venerated yet also treated as dangerous enemies. This tension was rationalized as a conflict between positive feelings for the living and negative feelings towards a corpse, or between the world of the living and the world of the dead. Yet Freud then pointed out that the relations between the living were themselves ambivalent. As he wrote in *Totem and Taboo*, 'In almost every case where there is an intense emotional attachment to a particular person we find that behind tender love there is a concealed hostility in the unconscious.'

Freud thought that such hostility was due to the disappointments and frustrations that are an inevitable part of our early relations with our caregivers. Demands for love would be left unsatisfied, expectations un-answered and sexual and romantic wishes thwarted. At an even more archaic level, Freud believed that our first relations with our caregivers always contain com-ponents of hatred, as a natural reaction to whatever is outside ourselves. We can't control what is outside us, and our parents wield a fearsome power over us. However much they love us, we are still more or less at their mercy at the start of life. Hatred is a basic reaction to those who have such power over us.

Problems in accepting these unconscious hostilities towards a loved one were once claimed as the most frequent cause of depressions. Unable to articulate our anger, we would become withdrawn and exhausted. Our energy would be sapped, as we inhibited our anger and sometimes turned this anger against ourselves. These once popular ideas are usually dismissed today with the observation that if the depressed person is asked whether they are angry, they will often say 'No.' Hence anger cannot be the cause of the depression. This simplistic criticism completely misses the point: the anger is not admitted to consciousness, and its traces will emerge only with detailed and lengthy analytic exploration.

Although few analysts would accept that this is the universal cause of despondency and dejection, blocked-out fury is certainly the cause of many instances of exhaustion and loss of interest in life. The link with exhaustion may be illustrated by the fact that often a baby will scream and cry and then suddenly, from one moment to the next, fall into the deepest sleep. We usually say that the infant has cried itself to sleep, but at times the sleep might be a defence against the pain of frustration or disappointment. Working with young children, I have observed on a few occasions how they can literally start to fall asleep in sessions when difficult material is coming to light. They will immediately forget what question has been asked or what theme was being discussed.

If hostility to those we love can be defended against with such vigour, in some cases it can be present in consciousness to serve a particular function. Speaking about the man who had left her, a woman remarked that 'If someone leaves you, it's worse than if they died. You know they are still alive. It's unbearable.' The only thing, she said, that stopped her from killing herself was her hatred of this man: 'I was about to do it,' she said, 'but my hatred kept me alive.' And the only way to get over him, 'to mourn him', she explained, 'was to denigrate him, to make him value-less, to kill him.' This use of hatred had a very precise role, and it evoked for her one of the central threads of her childhood. Growing up in a violent, strife-torn family with an alcoholic father and an aggressive, punitive mother, she said that the only thing that stopped her from going mad was her continuous hatred of her father: this hatred was what gave her a compass, an orientation in life. By focusing her hatred on him, she said, she kept her sanity.

Hatred may play this role as a focus, a point of consistency when all else seems unstable and liable to collapse. But hatred – whether it is conscious or not – can also complicate the mourning process quite seriously. Loss and bereavement do not always allow a ventilation of the feelings we might have repressed, and in general hostility to the dead is not well tolerated by us. It is far easier to express anger with the living, as we see when a stormy relationship suddenly becomes idealized by one partner after the death of the other. All the friction and turbulence seem to be miraculously airbrushed away, to leave an icon of saintliness in place of the dead partner. We find this obstruction fre-quently when we are exploring the lives of bereaved people: they become angry with colleagues, friends or lovers without linking this displacement consciously to their loss. Undertakers, doctors or hospital staff may also be recruited as targets, and time and time again we see the emergence of an 'enemy' in that person's circle after a significant loss. The anger is displaced on to someone else.

We can see this process clearly in a dream described by the writer Joan Didion after her husband John Gregory Dunne's death. She and her husband are flying to Honolulu and have assembled with many other people at Santa Monica Airport. Paramount Pictures have arranged planes for them and production assistants are distributing boarding passes. She boards the plane, but there is confusion. There is no sign of John. She worries there is a problem with his pass and decides to leave the plane and wait for him in the car. While waiting, she realizes that the planes are taking off one by one. Finally, she is alone on the tarmac. Her first thought in the dream is anger: John has boarded a plane without her. But the second thought transfers the anger: Paramount has not cared enough about them to put them on the plane together.

The partition of feelings at the end of this dream shows nicely how anger at a death cannot easily be directed at the one who has departed. It searches for another outlet, another target to displace itself to. We shift the anger away from the one we love. We can find another illustration of this process in the dream of a man mourning the death of someone he dearly loved. He dreamt repeatedly that he was furiously striking a leather pouch. Although he continued to batter it in the dream, he was also aware that this object 'wasn't the real target'. This realization, staged within the dream itself, would allow him to engage more clearly with his anger at the dead.

Didion's dream also suggests something else. In the move of the dreamer's reproach from her husband to Paramount, don't we see the necessity to blame something more than him? In the same way that some might blame fate or destiny, isn't this reproach directed to the symbolic* universe itself, represented here by the anonymous film company? Paramount is in the place of the agency pulling all the strings, arranging everything, in charge: what analysts would call the big Other. The departure of her husband is not simply a matter between the two of them but will involve this symbolic agency itself.

Situations of loss and separation often involve appeals to this mysterious higher power. The American analyst Martha Wolfenstein noticed how some of the children she worked with would make bargains with fate. In one case, a girl's father had a heart-attack when she was eight. She then developed compulsive rituals to distance any bad thoughts or words that might come into her mind. Being good meant for her that nothing bad would happen. When the father died six years later, it was as if fate had failed to keep its side of the bargain, and so she herself was released from it. She became promiscuous and gave up her previous diligence at school.

Displacements of our feelings are especially apparent in the hatred that often emerges towards a surviving parent. After her father's death, a woman could think of little else but her fury at her mother. This rage was

* Here, and in what follows, the term *symbolic* is used in its analytic sense: it refers to the order of language, representation and law which is imposed on us, rather than symbolism as such.

perplexing to her, as she had imagined their relations to be good. Beyond the rage that the mother, unlike the father, had 'escaped death', there was, she said, also a hatred here of her mother as being the one 'somehow responsible' for her love for the deceased. In another case, a similar hatred vented on the mother after the father's death was linked by the patient to her father's hatred of the mother: she had simply taken over his aggressive passion, identifying herself with his position. We might guess here that giving up the hatred would have meant, at some level, giving up the father.

We can also find many cases where the rage unleashed at a loss is linked to a change in the constellation of the family. A woman in her mid-fifties was terrified at the sudden pangs of fury she experienced after the death of her younger brother. The siblings had been brought up by the mother after the father had left during her second pregnancy, and the brother had become the object of all the mother's idealizations: he was the most beautiful, the most intelligent, the most successful. This untarnished image was never contested by the sister, and its role became clearer during her analysis. Faced with the mother's long bouts of misery and the string of anonymous men she would be forced to watch the mother entertain during her childhood, the brother's image took on a privileged position. In effect, it acted as a barrier between herself and her mother. Like the hatred described by the patient we discussed earlier, it functioned as an anchoring point in an unstable and precarious universe.

Once the brother's image was no longer present,

there was nothing to place between herself and her mother. This left her open to the question of what she was for the mother, and the contingent, threatened aspect of her own existence would come painfully into focus. Her feelings here oscillated between fury at the brother and an acute sense of dread and anguish linked to the mother. Although her anger at the brother for dying was unpalatable to her, it was strangely more grounding, she said, than the sense of anguish. This sort of feeling is often described by those whom a loss leaves alone with someone else: usually a parent. When one parent dies, there is no barrier to separate the child from the other parent, and one response to this can be the sense of anguish which signals that a barrier has been removed. There is not only the anger at the person for leaving, but the anger for having left us *with someone else*.

This rage we feel towards the dead can be devastating in both mourning and melancholia. It can get in the way of the work of mourning, confronting us with our fundamental ambivalence towards the one we've lost. These mixed feelings make us feel guilt, and so we may find that we chastise ourselves for what we could or should have done: we should have called or visited more often, been more agreeable, offered more help in some situation, and so on. Freud believed that it was this degree of ambivalence rather than the intensity of positive feelings towards the lost loved one that was the decisive factor in mourning. The more robustly we have tried to repress these ambivalent feelings previously in our relation with the person we have lost, the more they will interfere with the work of mourning. It was even argued by some post-Freudians that a mourning would only truly be over when the mourner could acknowledge their delight at the death of the one they loved.

Although Freud didn't hold such an extreme view, his idea of what gets in the way of mourning is quite radical. He is arguing, after all, that the decisive factor is not the strength of our attachment to the one we have lost. It isn't love, but the mixture of love and hate that matters. We'll have difficulties in mourning not because we loved someone too much, as common sense might suggest, but because our hatred was so powerful. Perhaps it is the very effort to separate the love and hate that incapacitates the mourner, leaving them trapped in a painful and devastating limbo that can take the form of exhaustion or panic.

In a case described by the psychoanalyst Helene Deutsch, a man went into analysis suffering from a variety of unexplained physical symptoms and a compulsive weeping which seemed to occur without any precipitating cause. Some years before, his mother had died and, hearing the news, he had left at once for the funeral, yet had felt no emotion at all. He tried to recall the treasured memories of her, yet even then he could not feel the suffering he wished for. He began to blame himself for not having mourned, and often thought of his mother in the hope that he might weep.

The analysis revealed that he had had an intense hatred of her from his infancy, which had been revived later in life. Her death produced the reaction 'She has left me', with all its accompanying anger. Instead of a sense of grief, there was only a coldness and indifference due to the interference of the hostile impulses. His guilt was generating the physical symptoms through which, Deutsch thought, he was identifying with her illness year after year. The compulsive weeping was the subsequent expression of his feeling, yet isolated from the thoughts about the death of his mother. It had been split off due to the strength of the ambivalence.

This kind of unconscious conflict gives the clue to many apparently unmotivated depressions, which are in fact the expression of emotional reactions once withheld and remaining latent ever since. They might emerge on the same day of the week or time of year that a loss had taken place in the past, yet the link is not made consciously. All we experience is the sadness and feeling of emptiness. Note how this is different from the clinical picture of melancholia where all the blame is focused on the self. In melancholia, this hatred will ravage the person's own ego, which has now become equated with the hated, unforgiven love object. The self is treated mercilessly.

———

The physical symptoms of Deutsch's patient mimicked those of his mother's illness, and this sort of identification is present to some extent in every mourning process. In melancholia it is pervasive, since the self is entirely swallowed up in an identification with the lost loved one. But in a general sense, we always identify with the ones we have lost. After his father died, a five-year-old boy would fit himself into a suitcase in the corner of the room, where he would remain motionless. When a friend asked his mother what he was doing, she replied that he was just sitting in a suitcase. Yet, as he saw clearly many years later, he had created his own private coffin, an enclosed space where he could act out an identification with the beloved father whom he had last seen in a coffin.

Describing the funeral of her mother, a woman said that as the hole was being dug in the earth, every strike of the spade felt like a strike deep within her own chest. She felt as if she were with the coffin being lowered into the ground. And the actress Billie Whitelaw writes of carrying pills with her when her son was on the brink of death, so she could follow him if he died. These are examples of homeopathy with the dead: we inhabit their space, taking on aspects of their behaviour, mannerisms, and even their ways of looking at the world.

In the early days of psychoanalysis, Josef Breuer observed a strange phenomenon with his patient Anna O. One day she told him there was a problem with her eyes: she knew she was wearing a brown dress, but she was seeing it as blue. Yet when checked with visual test-sheets, she could distinguish all the colours correctly. It turned out that the key detail lay in the material of the dress. During the same period a year previously she had been making a dressing-gown for her father during his fatal illness. This gown had been made from the same material as the dress she was now wearing, yet had been blue, not brown. Her visual disturbance, then, was both a kind of blocked memory and an identification with her father; as the one wearing the blue garment, she had in effect taken his place.

Such identifications can take many forms. In one case, a woman found herself rubbing the towel a second time over a dish that she had already dried, echoing her late father's habit of endlessly cleaning his shoes during his depression. They can also take more positive forms. A woman mourning her husband not long after his death noted how, when confronted with a problem, 'I deliberately looked at this in a way that my husband might have done had he been alive. I was surprised that I could honestly face and deal with it in a way I never could have previously.' In another case, after the loss of her husband, a woman took over his business, which became the main pursuit of her life. She turned it into an even more successful enterprise, emulating not only her husband's interests but his ways and methods of handling business matters.

If this is an example of the kind of identification we find in mourning, in melancholia something different will happen. As the psychoanalyst Edith Jacobson pointed out, the melancholic might, instead of taking over the ideals and pursuits of the husband, blame herself endlessly for her inability to carry out his business or for having ruined him, unaware that these self-reproaches unconsciously referred not to herself but to him. In one of Abraham's cases, a woman endlessly accused herself of being a thief, when in fact it was her deceased father who had been imprisoned for larceny. The identifications have this persistent accusatory quality.

These melancholic identifications have, as we've seen, a pervasive character. In one case, a melancholic man would spend his days visiting every single place in

London he imagined his dead sibling to have visited. It was as if he were completely identified with the departed, looking at the world exclusively from the latter's place. This is reminiscent of the experiences described by Lenin. After the execution of his elder brother Alexander, Lenin tried to learn all he could about the latter's life in St Petersburg, gathering information and reading everything Alexander had read, as if to do so through his eyes. Whereas Nikolai Chernyshevski's utopian novel *What Is to Be Done?* had made little impression on him when he had read it earlier, when he now re-read this book that had been so important for Alexander it had a powerful impact on him. This would have a huge effect on his life, as if his political career were formed, in part, around an identification with his dead brother.

A more recent example can be found in the Dutch film *The Vanishing*, directed by George Sluizer. It tells the story of a man searching for his abducted wife, who disappears one day when they stop at a motorway service station. The abductor watches his efforts to find her and, at the end of the film, offers him the opportunity to learn her fate. Desperate to know, he allows himself to be drugged, so as finally to solve the mystery of what happened to her. When he wakes up, he finds that he has been buried alive. His passion to re-find her covered over a profound identification with her: solving the mystery was in fact an alibi for wanting to join her. He put himself literally in the place of the lost object, with lethal consequences.

Similarly, in the film *Random Hearts*, Harrison Ford

and Kristin Scott Thomas play two characters whose spouses die in a plane crash. As the story unravels, it turns out that the spouses had been travelling together: they were going to Miami not on business but to continue their longstanding affair. Ford becomes obsessed with finding out everything about the relationship: where they went, what they did, which hotel rooms they stayed in and so on. As his morbid quest gathers momentum, he increasingly involves Scott Thomas, almost forcing her to share his obsession. As they visit the places where their spouses had conducted their romance, they become lovers themselves, as if they had come to inhabit the place of the dead. An incidental photograph of the two of them in a club before they become lovers is printed in a newspaper, yet it is not long before this 'untruth' becomes truth. It is as if they are being powerfully pushed into the place of the dead by a structure that is beyond them. They have ended up taking the place of the dead lovers.

Such unconscious identifications are far more common than we might think. We often hear of someone dying not long after the death of a loved one, especially after decades of marriage: we could think of the singer Johnny Cash or the politician James Callaghan, both of whom passed away soon after the death of their beloved wives. Grief is no longer included as a cause of death on death certificates, as it once was, but there is little doubt that in many cases the surviving partner wishes literally to join their lost love. In some cases this takes the form of a conscious wish, but it is just as often the result of unconscious forces. As in *Random Hearts*, there is a sense that a higher power, some force or destiny, is pushing the characters into an identification with the dead.

We also often learn of people's sense that they are doomed to repeat the life history of a deceased parent or family member, perhaps because of feelings of responsibility for their death. The psychoanalyst George Pollock thought that people's sense of a destiny often emerges when a parent or sibling has died when the person is young. They feel responsible for the death or illness, and so feel doomed to share the same fate. Van Gogh's experience illustrates this. He was named after a sibling predecessor who had died before his birth. He would often pass his brother's tombstone, and was inscribed in the parish register under the same number as his brother: twenty-nine. He would later commit suicide on the twenty-ninth day of July.

Another example is that of the psychoanalyst Marie Bonaparte, a Greek princess who was one of the first generation of Freudians and who also happened to have been the occasional baby-sitter of Prince Philip. Bonaparte's mother had died of TB at the age of twenty-two when Marie was one month old. She had been told that her birth had been paid for with her mother's life. Given the same name, Marie would become convinced that she too would share that fate. She began to develop symptoms that mimicked those of TB: she lost appetite and weight, contracted frequent respiratory infections and had bloody mucus in her throat.

Ignoring these identifications can be catastrophic. It can blind one to the danger of a suicide or gradual giving up of the will to live. It may also obscure the true meaning of a patient's symptoms, which may be mimicking those of a lost loved one. Yet, sadly, both medicine and psychology remain dangerously oblivious to these so common occurrences. Medicine doesn't want to know anything about the wish to die. And psychology tends to shy away from the Freudian idea of identification with the lost object. Yet example after example shows that this is a basic human response to loss. Either we take traits from the one we have lost, singular features that remain part of us, or, as in the melancholic case, we take everything. As the American analyst Bertram Lewin put it, the melancholic punishes the lost loved one in effigy, yet it is their own self which has *become* this effigy.

Curiously, the very process by which Freud character-ized melancholic identification was later used to describe the actual constitution of the human self. Our egos, he wrote, are made up of all the leftover traces of our abandoned relationships. Each broken relationship leaves its stamp on us, and our identity is a result of the building up over time of these residues. It's less 'You are what you eat' than 'You are what you've loved.' This gives a real twist to the earlier theory. Just when it seemed that the serious pathological state of melancholia had been explained, the same theory was being used to describe the most basic features of our identity. Was the building up of our ego really a melancholic process? Or could there be a subtle difference in the mechanism?

The idea of building our egos out of abandoned relationships certainly rings true. When we experience a break or disappointment in our involvement with someone we love, we often take on some of their attributes: a tone of voice, a taste for a certain food or even a way of walking. It's as if we remain trapped inside their images. This process is represented graphically in John Carpenter's film *The Thing*. An alien life-form starts to take over the members of a scientific team in a remote Arctic research station. As it pursues its colonizing aim, it takes possession not only of humans but of dogs and spiders, combining their bodies in horrific hybrids. At the end of the film, when the alien is finally destroyed, we see it decompose into each of the images it has donned until that moment: the individual members of the team, the dog, the spider are all paraded before our eyes in the agony of the alien's death throes. This terrifying moulting of images gives the model of the human ego, constructed from all those we have identified with, all those we have become.

But why should we see this process as characteristic of melancholia rather than mourning? There must be a difference first of all in terms of the self-reproach that Freud had set at the heart of melancholia. The identifications that build up our egos do not necessarily involve an attack on ourselves. We could also argue that perhaps the ego is built up not simply through our experience of loss, but through the *registration* of loss. The key feature here is the fact that a loss has been processed and represented. A loss, after all, always requires some kind of recognition, some sense that it has been witnessed and made real. That's why so much effort is made today to commemorate and mark traumatic events of the past, from the horrors of the Great War to the injustice and violence in a country such as South Africa. The Truth and Reconciliation Commission, after all, was less about punishing the perpetrators than about recognizing and registering their crimes. A separation, perhaps, only becomes a loss when it is registered.

Let's take an example here. A young couple fall in love and become engaged. The man goes to visit his family and tells them the good news of the engagement. As he is returning, he learns that his fiancée has been killed in a tragic accident. Yet when he expects to be able to share his grief with his friends and family, he realizes that none of them had ever actually met his lost loved one. He had only mentioned her to them very recently, and so he is faced with the problem of mourning someone who had not existed for those around him. No one else knew her. We see here a very particular situation. There has been a tragedy, but he feels the immense difficulty of registering this. When he went to meet her parents later on, he was in the strange situation of being the man she had been engaged to, yet whom they had neither met nor heard of.

In another case, a woman conducted a long relationship with a man in secret over several years. They knew each other intimately, yet, since they were both married, they shared the facts of their affair with no one. As they often emphasized to each other, secrecy was crucial. When the man withdrew from the relationship, mourning seemed impossible. How could she convey what had happened when, in a sense, the relationship had had no existence for those around her? In situations such as this, and in the case we mentioned above, there is the real problem of the absence of a third party. We suddenly become aware of the fact that we need other people not just to share our feelings with, but actually to confirm our own experiences, to make us sure that we have really lived them.

Survivors of the concentration camps reported a common nightmare of returning home yet finding no one to notice them or believe what had happened to them. It wasn't only the horrors of the camps that would return to torment them, but the agonizing feeling that there was no one there to authenticate their experience. Without some form of third party, we have no anchor, no way of believing in the authenticity of what we have gone through. Although Hamlet knows perfectly well that his uncle is guilty of murder, is it an accident that he has to wait for the Ghost to appear before passing a death sentence on Claudius?

This kind of triangle, in which we need the presence of a third party to confirm what we feel for someone else, is exploited relentlessly by daytime television. Countless chat shows invite guests to declare their sentiments on air for someone they love or, in some cases, wish to separate from: people begin marriages or end them, confront parents or reconcile with them, confess sins or swear fidelity. Crucially, all these performative actions, in which speech is used *to do* something, such as swearing or confessing, take place on a stage, in front of an audience. These shows rely on the principle that words ultimately require someone to sanction them beyond their immediate addressee, in the same way that a marriage or a funeral ceremony requires the symbolic presence of a priest or some sort of facilitator. In many cases, someone who has experienced a loss will seek out a third party – perhaps an analyst or therapist – in order to perform this authenticating function.

In the mourning process, this kind of sanction is often represented in dreams. There is a significant difference between those dreams which involve the mourner's interactions with the dead or departed, and those in which the mourner talks *about* that person to someone else. Some time after her mother's death, a woman caught in a painful and protracted grief dreamt that she was telling a faceless third party that her mother had died. Although she could not fill in any detail of this listening figure, the dream marked a moment of change for her. By introducing a basic triangulation, it showed that the loss was being registered, transformed into a message to be transmitted to someone else and accepted, at some level, by herself.

2

We have seen how Freud distinguished mourning and melancholia. In mourning, our memories and hopes linked to the one we've lost are run through, and each is met with the judgement that the person is no longer there. This process of surveying and re-shuffling thoughts and images will eventually exhaust itself, and the mourner will choose life over death. In pathological or complicated mourning, this process is arrested, due primarily to the presence of powerful feelings of hate mixed with our love for the deceased. In melancholia, the unconscious hatred of the one we've lost twists back to submerge us: we rage against ourselves as we once raged against the other, due to our unconscious identification with them. We have become what we could not bear to give up.

How, then, did the psychoanalytic community respond to Freud's essay? Surprisingly, everyone disagreed. The two most important replies were first from the Berlin analyst Karl Abraham and then, some years later, from Melanie Klein. Both Klein and Abraham thought that Freud's polarization of mourning and melancholia was too rigid. They questioned the very distinction between them that had been pivotal to Freud's argument. Although they developed different theories here, what linked Klein's and Abraham's perspectives was a basic observation: that our earliest relations with our caregivers in infancy begin in ambivalent settings. Love and hate are always directed towards the same people, however much we might try to separate out our emotions or to deny them. Although Freud had of course discussed this, they felt he hadn't taken it far enough. He had confined the conflict of emotions to the state of pathological mourning, they thought, when it was in fact central to all forms of mourning.

This meant that when we lose a loved one, reproach is always going to be present, and so, they claimed, there was a continuum between mourning, pathological mourning and melancholia. Equally, the kind of internalization of the lost loved one that Freud had found in melancholia was in fact a feature of all forms of mourning as well. This internalization, Abraham claimed, was a cannibalistic one, as if the lost object was incorporated through the mouth. Although this may seem a strange idea, we should remember how infants' first relation with their caregiver is through feeding. Many languages have expressions like 'I want to eat you up' to signify affection and love, and problems in love may well be associated with changes in one's relation to food, from loss of appetite to bulimic binges. In some rare cases of psychosis, this imaginary wish to incorporate becomes real: the loved one may be actually killed and then eaten. However infrequent this may be in reality, the unconscious appeal of this kind of incorporation is reflected in the popular fascination with Hannibal Lecter, the murderous gourmet who feasts on his victims.

Separations and losses are often marked by changes

in eating behaviour, showing how the very basic mechanisms of swallowing and spitting out define, in some sense, our relation to those we love. When the anthropologist Jack Goody was doing his fieldwork with the Lodagaa of West Africa, he was puzzled at the way that mourning women were held back at the funeral from the body of their loved one. Why, he wondered, was a distance so necessary? The answer he received was simple: to restrain them from biting the corpse. Reviewing the range of funeral customs in different cultures, one anthropologist could say that the single most widespread element was the role accorded to eating. Mourning his beloved Patroklos, Achilles can still encourage his companions to feast, and food remains essential at wakes and funerals.

The variety of our ways of incorporating is fascinating, and it ranges from biting to sucking, swallowing to sniffing, listening to looking. A woman suffering from an eye disease which had begun late in life explained, in her analysis, how as a child she had used blinking as a way of holding on to other people. When she saw her father on his periodic visits home, she would rapidly clamp her eyes shut, believing that this would 'seal him in'. She could hold on to him by enclosing him with the action of her eyelids. Later she would blink at school when she had to learn something, to allow her to 'hold it in'. By closing the eyes, she thought, she would be able to retain what would otherwise escape her.

Strange as it may seem, inhalation is another route used to incorporate. Otto Fenichel noticed this in the early days of psychoanalysis, remarking how some people spoke of their wish to suck the other in through their nostrils. Adults in love will occasionally experience this peculiar urge, knowing full well how absurd it is, yet still feeling a compulsion to suck the other person inside of them. Sometimes, after a break-up, a lover will even purchase the perfume used by their ex and sniff it in a private, painful ritual. The psychoanalyst Colette Soler made a very precise observation here. She pointed out that the early Freudians had been too quick to interpret what they saw as the sadistic side of such activities. Biting, nipping, scratching, sniffing and all the other incorporative practices at the dawn of our lives may in fact signify ways of trying to apprehend the mystery of the body of the caregiver: what is this vast Other that is there at the centre of our lives? Confronted with an enigma, children use all the oral and muscular techniques at their disposal to try to grasp what this Other is.

A man very much in love with his partner spoke about some of the impulses he had when they were in bed. After they had made love, he would lie next to her, with the urge, he said, 'not to penetrate her, but to somehow envelop her'. He didn't know exactly what this meant, but he knew that it wasn't the same thing as sex. He wanted to 'possess her, to take her inside me', and at the same time to map every point on his own body with hers. He imagined lying on her in such a way that every square inch of her body was touching his. This, he acknowledged, was impossible, and the thought of this impossibility haunted him. As he would pinch, squeeze and inhale her, he experienced an oral greed to take in more, yet at the same time felt strongly a sense that he 'didn't know what to do' with her body. The little attacks on her flesh could be understood as a kind of sadism but seem more linked to the effort to apprehend the Other's body as described by Soler. They were like limit points, markers of what he wished for yet could never possess.

Now, Abraham had been in a dialogue with Freud about the mechanisms of grieving for some time before the publication of *Mourning and Melancholia*. Although he had authored a number of articles dealing with these issues, it was his *Short Study of the Development of the Libido* published in 1924 that explored the question of loss most extensively. Reading this text it is difficult to ignore the fact that rumours of Freud's imminent death from cancer had been circulating shortly before Abraham put pen to paper, and a strange mechanism emerges in the Berlin analyst's prose: he repeatedly makes statements like 'psychoanalysis has thrown no light on [mourning] in healthy people and in cases of transference neurosis', a claim which is astounding given the sophistication of Freud's paper. He then invariably follows such statements – and there are plenty of them – with an obsequious reference to Freud, a rhythm which bears uncanny testimony to the very phenomenon of ambivalence that he argues is so crucial to the mourning process.

This ambivalence is found by Abraham at the heart of all forms of mourning, which he sees as derivatives of melancholia. In its basic melancholic form, the child's hatred of the mother – intensified by early disappointments coincident with the oral sadistic phase

— can swamp their love, and they find themselves unable either to wholly hate or wholly love her. This impasse would be felt as a profound hopelessness, which Abraham believed lay behind many of the depressive states experienced by both children and adults. The early relations with the mother here will be shaped by oral sadistic drives and the melancholic will try desperately to escape these, mainly by turning them against himself. This reversal will generate the self-reproaches that had so intrigued Freud.

When we lose someone later in life, Abraham thought, our childhood situation will always be revived. We are catapulted back to our original ambivalent relation to the mother. Thus, in Abraham's logic, self-reproach is ultimately a reproach to the mother, the first object of our ambivalence. But self-reproach, he adds, may also have other sources. A son's complaints about himself may turn out to echo exactly the mother's complaints about him or that of one of the parents about the other. The attack on the parent present in the reproach may actually mirror an attack by a third party on that person: a son's self-reproaches may echo those of the mother to the father, for example. All of these possibilities broaden Freud's model of self-reproach.

Abraham thought that we unconsciously experience loss as an anal process of ejection, which is then followed by our wish to incorporate orally what is no longer there. Our elementary bodily functions of incorporating and expelling are being used to make sense of loss. Both of these oral and anal processes have subdivisions: to expel and destroy on one level for the anal process and to retain and control on the other, and sucking and pleasure on one level for the oral process with biting and destruction on the other. The one we love is expelled like excrement and then devoured in phantasy. Once the melancholic's thirst for vengeance has been turned against himself, it will torment him until the sadistic tendencies have somehow been appeased and the love object (the mother) removed from the danger of being destroyed. Thus the mourning process ends when the subject has been liberated from the object, a process which is equated with shitting it out.

If these ideas may seem unfamiliar, we find bodily processes brought into play time and time again at moments of loss or separation. In one case, a man's family became increasingly worried about his hoarding tendencies. Although he had always had an interest in collecting, from a certain point onwards he refused to throw anything away. Magazines, newspapers, packaging and other detritus would accumulate so that there was little room left in his home for anything else. Nothing could be discarded. Emptying his bowels seemed an equally impossible task, and he suffered from a serious, chronic constipation. All of this had started in the weeks following the death of his father, as if, unable to accept the loss, he had to make sure that everything in his world was retained. Loss was simply no longer possible.

Klein continued Abraham's research on melancholia, agreeing with him that melancholia and mourning were forms of the same structure. Like Abraham, she disagreed with the common idea that mourning, as opposed to melancholia, involved an unalloyed love. Losing someone, she argued, will revive all the earlier losses that one has experienced and attributed to one's own destructive impulses. If someone is lost through separation or death, a powerful current of our mental life makes us feel responsible for the loss. Working with survivors of the Hiroshima bomb, Robert Lifton noted how the 'A-bomb orphans' found it difficult to suppose that the death of their parents did not have a link to their own malevolence: as one child said to him, 'We did nothing bad – and still our parents died.'

Klein believed that the idea of being somehow responsible for the loss of or injury to our loved ones will powerfully influence our mental life. When we are separated from someone through death or estrangement, this will undermine any feelings of the secure possession of our internalized representations of those we love and will revive earlier anxieties about injured and damaged objects. Hence for Klein, 'A successful reinstating of the external love object which is being mourned, and whose introjection is intensified through the process of mourning, implies that the loved internal objects are restored and regained.' This will draw on libidinal phantasies and desires, crucial in sublimation, and it means that one's whole internal world has to be re-created. We have to assure ourselves that we have not done irreparable damage to the objects that matter to us.

What would such a process involve? Klein thought that in our earliest relation with our caregivers, we separate good and bad, frustrating and gratifying. Instead of relating to a breast or mother that is both good and bad, frustrating and gratifying, we relate to separate breasts and mothers: the good and the bad. It is only with the working through of this separation that we come to appreciate that good and bad are attributes that qualify one and the same object. Once we realize this, we will feel guilty for our aggressions against what we now know to be our loved object. A phase of sorrow and concern will follow as we try to make amends, and Klein called this process the depressive position.

Mourning, for Klein, means that the straits of the depressive position will have to be run through with each significant loss we experience. This involves the painful realization that loved and hated aspects of the mother or parts of her body are not separate entities but aspects of the same person and will generate feelings of sadness and guilt. Hence we will try to make amends, a process Klein termed reparation. Subsequent attempts at reparation are understood as efforts to overcome mourning. If early struggles around the loss of the mother had not been dealt with, depressive illness is more likely to ensue. As for self-reproach, this is taken to be the vehicle both of harm done to the object by hostile impulses and of a more fundamental hatred of one's drives: in Klein's view, a hatred of one's own hatred. This may be even more archaic than the previous form of hatred: the ego's very existence is threatened by the unleashing of one's destructivity, threatening the ruin of the ego's love objects.

Klein's ideas here resonate powerfully with clinical experience. When we receive a recently bereaved person in analysis, we often see a peculiar phenomenon. If their last surviving parent, for example, has just died, we may then witness a long process where what they talk about is the death of the *other* parent. It's as if an earlier loss must be worked through before they are able to start speaking about the more recent loss. This can be bewildering for the clinician, if they expect that a recently bereaved person will want to talk immediately about their recent loss. They may even suggest this to the patient or feel that the recent loss is being avoided or denied. Following Klein's logic, however, each loss revives earlier losses, and so these must be run through first. As the writer Cheryl Strayed observed after her mother's death, she had expected that 'the single act of her death would constitute the only loss . . . No one told me that in the wake of that grief other griefs would ensue.'

The other clinical phenomenon that Klein captured so brilliantly was splitting. Freud makes no mention of this in his essay, yet Klein notes the way that good and bad can be absolutely polarized in mourning states. After a loss, for example, memories or dreams of the lost loved one can represent them as either all good, completely idealized and positive or, on the contrary, all bad, the incarnation of evil itself. This often disturbs the bereaved person, since they experienced no such splitting consciously in their day-to-day relations with the loved one prior to the loss. But now representations of the loved one seem to be split between these two extremes of good and bad. This also often happens when couples separate: the ex is vilified as a merciless demon or, on the contrary, transformed into an unimpeachable angel. There seems to be no middle ground.

The idea of making reparation that Klein saw as so essential to the mourning process is also common to many situations of loss and grief. The child, she thought, will desperately try to make amends for the damage they believe they have inflicted on their love object. When a real loss occurs, the menace of their own murderous drives suddenly becomes more pronounced, as if they had been responsible, and so reparation is reactivated. In analysis, we often hear dreams during the mourning period in which a damaged body is repaired or mended. One man, after his mother's death, dreamt of a whale with a huge gash in its side, which he stitched up with a harpoon cable. The ubiquity of these motifs of repair fits nicely with Klein's theory, although, as we will see, there are certainly other ways of explaining them.

Klein's work stands out in its sensitivity to the phenomena surrounding bereavement: the often rigid splitting into good and bad polarities, the presence of manic states, and the frequency of dreams of damaging and repairing a body are all remarkably clear in such cases. It is quite tempting to imagine that Klein was inspired, certainly in her research during the 1930s, not only by her work with such patients, but also perhaps by her own personal experience. Having already lost her parents, her sister Sidonie and her brother Emanuel, her son Hans died in April 1934. It was only a few months later, in August, that she delivered the first version of her ground-breaking paper on the origin of manic-depressive states to the psychoanalytic congress at Lucerne.

—

If we try to amplify Freud's theory with the ideas of Abraham and Klein, we still have a problem. Whatever we make of these psychoanalytic theories, they still leave something out, something so important that it becomes a real puzzle to understand its absence. What happened to the social dimension of mourning? The analytic perspectives we have reviewed seem to dispense completely with the role of other people. Mourning is treated as a private event and not as a public, social process. This absence becomes all the more curious when we realize that in the years leading up to the draft of *Mourning and Melancholia*, Freud had been steeped in the writings of the Cambridge anthropologists, who had plenty to say about precisely the social aspects of mourning. Writers such as James Frazer devoted hundreds of pages to describing how indigenous societies involved the community in mourning their dead, and Freud was to use much of this data himself in works like *Totem and Taboo*.

While social responses to bereavement involve formalized public displays and the involvement of the community, the mourning described by Freud is an intensely private process. The individual is alone with their grief. Indeed, there are simply no references in his discussion to the participation of other people in the process of grieving, a feature that has continually baffled later commentators. Just a few years before the publication of *Mourning and Melancholia*, the sociologist Emile Durkheim had described mourning as less an individual process of grief than an imperative of the social group; less a movement of private feelings wounded by loss than a duty imposed by the community.

In his important 1965 survey *Death, Grief and Mourning*, the anthropologist Geoffrey Gorer drew attention to this omission, pointing out that every documented human society has mourning rituals which involve public displays. Besides funeral rituals, even dress codes could reveal that someone had been bereaved, whom they had lost and how long it had been since the loss. Black clothes would be worn in many Western countries, although early Christians were in fact instructed to wear white to distinguish themselves from the heathen. In Syria, light blue is the colour of mourning, while it is white for Hindus and for the Chinese. Other details of colour or style would indicate whether the loss had been of a parent or of a sibling, when it had taken place, and further information about the loss. These outward signs would help to inscribe the mourner within a shared, public space.

Gorer and others argued that the decline of public mourning rituals in the West was linked to the mass slaughter of the First World War. The surplus of the dead – and bereaved – was far more extreme and concentrated than in earlier warfare, and so profound changes were forced on society. What sense would it make for a community to mourn each dead soldier when the corpses were hardly even countable?

Significantly, it was precisely during this period that Freud began writing his essay. In that sense, the understanding of mourning as an individual problem came at just the time that it was becoming more distanced from community life. The outward manifestations of mourning were becoming more and more obscured as grief moved inwards. In the majority of cases, modern Western mourners do not follow a set dress code or manifest their pain outwardly. Instead, they are supposed to work it through themselves, as if mourning were solely a private process.

Jackie Kennedy's stoicism at the funeral of her husband is perhaps the most famous example of this image of a contained grief. Even though the funeral was a major public event, televised nationally for millions of viewers, there was no outpouring of grief, no tears or wailing. Those who had never even met the president certainly experienced these signs of emotion, but Jackie's calmness became emblematic of a grief that was internalized and not displayed. Although some saw this as a model of courage and fortitude, others shared the view of one commentator that it 'set mourning back a hundred years'.

The erosion of public mourning rituals continues today in many parts of the world that had not experienced the mass slaughter of the great wars. In African societies, the toll of AIDS has meant that mourning and burial rituals that have been practised for hundreds of years are now being abandoned or abridged. HIV-AIDS is now the leading cause of death for people aged between fifteen and fifty-nine in Tanzania and other countries. The sheer quantity of the dead means that it is no longer feasible to retain traditional ritual processes, and economic plight makes many such practices, such as the sacrifice of animals, impossible. We must ask what the consequences of this destruction of the social fabric will be. And what its consequences have been in the West, where mourning rituals have already collapsed.

There is an odd, paradoxical effect of this erosion. Where the great taboo of Victorian culture had been sex, Gorer thought that today it is death. We might object that in fact today we are continually assailed by images of violent death, in the cinema, on television, and in the media. But one could see, in turn, this ramification as a strict *consequence* of the disappearance of mourning rites. Without the symbolic support of mourning rites, images of death simply proliferate to the point of meaninglessness.

Most Western human beings in fact watch images of death every night in the TV shows about crime scene investigation and murder that fill up the evening programme schedule. It is amazing to realize that this is what most people do after work: they watch programmes in which someone dies and whose death is subsequently explained and made sense of. The fact that this is reiterated endlessly suggests that death is ultimately not something that can be made sense of. And that the increasingly violent images multiply in the absence of a symbolic framework that might mediate them.

It seems vital here to try to integrate the traditional psychoanalytic theories of mourning and an attention to the public, social dimension. This will allow us to deepen our understanding not only of the mourning process but of the consequences of the erosion of community mourning. How can we link the private and the public here, the personal and the social?

—

We find a clue to this problem in a remark made by Melanie Klein in her 1940 paper on mourning and its relation to manic-depressive states. Sometimes, she says, the mourning process can be aided if our internal objects – meaning one's unconscious representations of other people – are mourning with us. 'In the mourner's state of mind,' she writes, 'the feelings of his internal objects are also sorrowful. In his mind, they share his grief, in the same way as actual kind parents would. The poet tells us that "Nature mourns with the mourner."' This comment provides the crucial link between the personal and the social that we are looking for. It suggests that our own access to mourning can be helped if we perceive that other people are mourning too. This apparently simple point in fact opens up a wealth of questions and new perspectives on the mourning process.

In one of the most famous and earliest texts to deal with the question of mourning, the *Iliad*, we read of the dreadful blow dealt to Achilles by the death of his lover Patroklos. As the assembled crowd mourn the dead warrior, we learn that they are crying less for him than for the losses he brought to mind. The women lament his passing openly, while at the same time 'each one for her own sorrows', and the men 'each one remembering what he had left at home'. The public display of grief allows each individual to access their own losses. Such processes are not arbitrary additions to the public display of grief but a basic feature of them. Public mourning is there in order to allow private mourning to express itself. The lamentation for long-dead heroes that had such a precise place in Hellenistic culture had the function of providing a space for the bewailing of individual, private losses.

A woman mourning the death of her mother dreamt that she was trying on a dress and that her mother was pinning the hem like a seamstress. When she scrutinized the dress itself, she found it to be a heavy garment, like the national costume of her native country. This was the type of garment she had worn at school at times of ceremony, to recite poems or speeches to the glory of ancestors and departed heroes. Punctuating a difficult mourning process, the dream indicates not only the idea of her mother helping her to assume the role of mourner, but also the movement towards public display. Her own individual mourning passes through and is precipitated by this entry into the image of the set, public role of mourner.

Today's controversies over the phenomena of public grief are telling here. When Diana died, public responses verged on hysteria, leading cynics to claim that the tears were not real. Newspaper headlines refer to 'mourning sickness', mocking the 'crocodile tears' of today's public grief. They are not genuine tears for Diana or, in another example, the murdered Soham girls. But this cynicism totally misses the point. No one could seriously argue that these tears are *for* the dead figures themselves. Rather, it is precisely the public framework that allows people to articulate their own grief for other, unrelated losses. The thousands of letters that Dickens received after the death of his character Little Nell made him think that he had committed a real murder, yet it was surely the social, shared aspect of this fictional death that allowed each reader to access their own grief, even without knowing it. This is a basic function of public mourning rituals. The public facilitates the private.

Cynics today who complain of 'mourning sickness' fail to remember that for many centuries professional mourners would be hired for funerals. What sense could be made of this age-old practice unless we factored in the relation between public and private? As the professional mourners lamented and bewailed the passing of the dead, the mourners could access their own private grief. The public, ostentatious display of others was necessary for them to enter their own grief. The very fact that these hired hands were professionals signals the gap between public and private. If they were too close, perhaps the outward manifestations of sadness would seem less like signs, artificial elements that were well rehearsed. Without this artificial distance, the mourner remains in the same space as the dead, rather than being able to situate their loss within a different, more symbolic space.

Let's take another example. Mark Roseman's book *The Past in Hiding* tells the story of Marianne Ellenbogen, a young Jewish woman who survived underground in Nazi Germany. Roseman interviewed Ellenbogen when she was an elderly woman living in England in the 1980s. But his narrative does not rely simply on these interviews: he also draws on her contemporary diaries together with information gathered from a number of other sources. The book is rare in its bold handling of a difficult subject: what interests Roseman is less to paint a picture of heroism and valour than to examine the tensions between fiction and non-fiction in Marianne's own narrative. Her diaries from the war often tell a very different story from her later reconstructions, just as both of these sources sometimes conflict with external accounts.

As Roseman scrutinized the material, a pattern became clear. Where moments of separation were so traumatic as to be unbearable for Marianne, they would be rewritten using the memories of other people. Her own separation from her fiancé, for example, would be told using details of another separation she had heard about from friends. How could this strange phenomenon be understood? It is less a question of so-called false memory syndrome than of the principle of *borrowed mourning*: the stories that Marianne would substitute for the unspeakable points in her own narrative concerned someone else grieving a loss, together with little details about the circumstances of that loss. Although, as Roseman shows, these losses were not her own, can't we see them as tools that allowed her to mourn? She was able to make something from how other people had represented their own grief. And we could call this a *dialogue of mournings*.

A dialogue of mournings can have many effects. It can allow one person to actually start the mourning process proper, and it can provide the material necessary to represent their loss. As we read in Shakespeare's *Richard III*, 'If sorrow can admit society, / Tell o'er your woes again by viewing mine.' This process of 'viewing' can shed light on other phenomena, since it alerts us to the active effects of comparison. Finding a representation that echoes our own situation can initiate a mourning process, even if the *rhythm* of comparison is not always smooth. The time it takes a child to mourn is so often different from that of their widowed parent and can generate great bitterness. If the surviving parent remarries, many children resent what they see as the undue swiftness of the adult's mourning.

There can also be cases where the proximity of grief is felt as *too* close. Martha Wolfenstein discusses the blocked mourning of an adolescent girl, whose mother had died of a brain haemorrhage when she was fifteen. After the funeral, she found herself unable to cry, and was relieved to meet another girl who had experienced a similar reaction after the death of her own father. Yet the dialogue of mournings was inflected here with a sense of terror. She dreamt that her grandfather leaned close to her and said 'Let us mingle our tears.' Whether we agree with Wolfenstein or not that this menacing figure represented the father, the horror that the dream aroused in the daughter was clearly incestuous. Perhaps in this case the mother's death meant not just the loss of a loved parent but also being left alone with the surviving one. Manifesting sorrow could then only confirm the new and disturbing closeness between father and daughter: being united in grief meant, for her, a form of being united. Her anxiety was a signal of the danger of this incestuous desire.

If the comparison of mourning processes can be complex and multi-layered, what about those instances where the very possibility of comparison seems to be ruled out? The most evident – and perhaps the only – example of such a barrier in our culture is the Holocaust. When Sylvia Plath dared to use images of the Holocaust in her poem 'Daddy' to dramatize personal, autobiographical threads, the response was outrage and anger. If we take seriously the argument about the resonance between mournings, this produces a number of problems: in particular, the seal of prohibition on comparison that marks representations of the Holocaust prevents the pattern of mourning we have discussed from taking place. On a clinical level, this is a crucial point. Think of all those cases where a loss in a family has not been openly mourned. What consequences will this have, we can ask, on the children? How can they mourn if they are deprived of the very possibility of a dialogue of mournings?

This is the basic problem in that classic study of grief, *Hamlet*. Shakespeare's character has lost his father, murdered by his uncle Claudius, whom his mother subsequently marries. Gertrude is a mother who is unable to mourn: no sooner has her husband been removed than she opens her arms to another man. No mourning period is observed, no subjective loss is acknowledged or properly symbolized. It is only after the scene in the cemetery when Hamlet comes upon

Laertes grieving so ostentatiously for Ophelia that he is able to access his own mourning. Laertes mourns where Hamlet has not. But once Hamlet confronts him, the dialogue of mournings blocked by Gertrude can start to unravel.

This link of one person's mourning to another's is not confined to drama. A Harvard research project on grieving found that most of the widows interviewed had felt obliged to hide their tears. Just as the dying husband might have instructed his wife not to mourn for him, to save her from pain, so the bereaved mothers would try to save their children from the pain of loss by not mentioning the death. Yet how a parent has represented a loss is crucial for the mourning process: as we see again and again clinically, when a loss is not symbolized in a family history, it so often returns to haunt the next generation. Many of those investigating the lives of the children of Holocaust survivors claimed that the parent would put a massive premium on their child being happy and not confronting loss. This, of course, is not an isolated phenomenon and it occurs very widely: the more that a parent avoids engaging with losses in their own life, projecting an ideal of happiness and comfort on their child, the more the latter may try to reveal the suppressed truth.

In one case, a man prone to depressive moods began to use heroin, while at the same time daydreaming about his mother finding out. He also imagined a variety of appalling crimes which he would commit, until finally his mother would be forced to recognize that her child was a monster. He had grown up crushed by his mother's ideal image of him: nothing he ever did was wrong and no amount of misbehaviour would be viewed negatively. She had projected on to him the glorified image of her own father, whose death when she was a child had never been properly accepted by her. Growing up in the oppressive atmosphere of someone else's fantasy meant that he searched for his mother's hate, as a minimal sign of authenticity. As both Winnicott and Lacan noted, hatred may be difficult to bear, but at least it indicates something *real*. For the man in question, it would prove that at last he had been recognized for himself and not for some fantasy image that had been imposed on him.

This emergence of truth may take many forms, ranging from depressive states – to show the falsity of the parent's ideal image – to reveries and fictions. A writer described how she had discovered by chance that she had had a brother who had died when he was only a few days old, three years before her birth. Suddenly, she said, so many aspects of her own life were thrown into perspective. She had been obsessed with the idea of ghosts and these had featured repetitively in her childhood fiction. She had also imagined for years that she had a male double, a little boy whose image she would conjure up and dialogue with. Although her parents had never said a word to her about the dead brother, this unspoken secret was still transmitted and its unspokenness gave it an even more terrible weight.

It had been after overhearing a chance remark when she was ten that she had begun to do detective work, searching through family documents and papers for traces of the brother's existence. A strange thing happened when she finally found real, written evidence of his birth and death: within a few days of the discovery, her periods started. The family doctors were nonplussed at this bizarre biological turn: they had never seen a girl menstruate at such a tender age. Years later, during her analysis, she understood why her body had reacted in this spectacular way. The periods meant, after all, that she was a girl. By affirming her bodily femininity, it was as if she were removing herself from the shadow of the dead boy that had so haunted her past.

The place of knowledge here is crucial. Symbolizing a separation or death is a necessary part of being able to start thinking about it. During the dictatorship in Argentina, mothers of men and women who had disappeared – no doubt to be tortured and killed by the police and military – would assemble on Thursdays at a public monument to independence in one of Buenos Aires' main squares. Silently, they would circle the monument, each holding a handkerchief on which was inscribed the name of the missing child and the date of their disappearance. As the psychoanalyst Maud Mannoni pointed out, they were insisting on the minimal symbolic gesture that an inscription mark the dead or departed.

Such inscriptions are a rudimentary form of knowledge, indexing a death or separation rather than hiding it. Yet we so often hear in analytic practice of the weight placed upon a child by some knowledge about one of the parents that they have been told to keep to themselves: an infidelity, an impending separation, a crime. Having to keep the secret might make them faithful to the parent in question, but the pressure of retaining the secret can be ravaging. When it comes to questions of illness and death, this pressure can be just as acute. There may be an awareness of an impending death or knowledge of the true cause of death which is not shared, or, in other cases, an exclusion from the facts, as we often see when there has been a suicide in a family.

Geoffrey Gorer observed that it had become a commonplace by the mid-twentieth century to hide a patient's fatal diagnosis from them. Where the historian of childhood Philippe Ariès found a preparedness for death in earlier cultural testimonies, both he and Gorer saw the contemporary problem as precisely this relation of death to knowledge. Cultures tend to rationalize this troubling question in different ways. In Iran, for example, to receive tragic news of a death when alone or away from one's family is believed by some to lead to a specific form of illness, so Iranians abroad are often not told of a death until they return home months or even years later. This practice, however common, in no way lessens the adverse effect of being excluded from knowledge.

Contemporary Western culture inflects this problem of knowledge in its own way: where children were once gathered around a deathbed, today we hear increasingly of their separation. Ariès notes that until the eighteenth century no portrayal of a deathbed scene failed to include children. And where a parent decides it is for the good of the child to keep them away from a funeral, we may hear about it decades later with a sense of disappointment or resentment. This means that we have to add to Freud's argument about mourning. The relation of the bereaved to the dead person is one thing, but this will be affected by how those around the bereaved have responded to the loss. As humans, don't we need others to authenticate our losses? To recognize them as losses rather than to pass over them in silence? Don't we need, in other words, a dialogue of mournings?

—

Why would public display be necessary here? After a traumatic loss, we need to receive the message that something terrible has happened. If this seems obvious, think of the many cases where the only response is denial or blankness. To take one significant example, we probably all know of cases where a miscarriage is passed over in silence. At least 15 per cent of pregnancies end in miscarriage, and it is clear that society often gives little space for a mourning here. What is a tragedy for the mother and the father may be ignored or denied by others, blocking the designation of the event *as a loss*. Yet there is a vital human need to designate events symbolically.

In one case, after a miscarriage, a woman had a dream in which she was told that a tragedy had occurred. The whole dream took place as a performance, as if all the characters were acting. They tell her there is a 'cavity' inside her and the video monitors in the room in her dream evoked those next to her in the hospital when she miscarried. The loss here is moving towards being represented, and this representation is made public, woven into a broader structure. The way in which a private grief is transformed here into a kind of public performance suggests something about what art itself is about. What place, after all, do literature, theatre, cinema and the other visual and plastic arts have in human culture? Could their very existence be linked to the human necessity to mourn? And if so, how?

In an article developing Melanie Klein's ideas about aesthetics, the Kleinian analyst Hanna Segal makes a very simple but also barely noticed point about our experience of works of art. Although at some level we might believe that we 'identify' with the protagonists, there is also a process of identification with the creator, in the sense of someone who could make something out of an inferred experience of loss. As Segal puts it, they have created something 'out of chaos and destruction'. Reading a James Bond novel, we might think that we are identifying with the glamorous spy, but in fact, strange as it may seem, at a deeper level we are identifying with Bond's creator, Ian Fleming.

This may seem rather counter-intuitive, and we might certainly disagree with Segal's explanations, but at some level it rings true. The key here lies in the importance of exposure to the manifest mourning process of someone else. Segal goes on to argue that it is through 'identifying with the artist' that a successful mourning can be achieved, implying perhaps a more transitory experience of catharsis than the drawn-out work of mourning described by Freud. However, if we follow her approach and see all creative works as being products of the same mechanisms, the place of

86

the arts in a culture takes on a new sense: *as a set of instruments to help us to mourn*. The arts exist to allow us to access grief, and they do this by showing publicly how creation can emerge from the turbulence of a human life. In our unconscious use of the arts, we have to go outside ourselves to get back inside.

This was already a motif in Plato's *Republic*, where we can read how 'poets gratify and indulge the natural desire to weep and lament to our heart's content, which in our private misfortune we forcibly restrain.' When critics argue today about the social function of art and how it has been lost, they miss this crucial point. The true social function of art, perhaps, is to present models of creation. And that is why the diversity of each artistic act is so crucial.

This fact alone can encourage each of us to create for ourselves, in however modest a way. When today's schoolchildren are taught emotional literacy, the idea is to help them to express their emotions. They are taught a language to articulate what they are feeling and what others are feeling. This well-intentioned practice is sadly tantamount to brainwashing, in the sense that it imposes a language on the individual and coerces them to use it in place of their own unique ways of expressing themselves. The casualties here are the subjects of literature, drama and art for a very precise reason. These do not force a pre-set language on children but expose them to a variety of ways of creating, from Shakespeare to Picasso, from J. K. Rowling to Tracey Emin. Children are thus confronted with the ways that individuals have responded in their own unique fashion to the experience of frustration, sadness and loss. And, as we have seen with the idea of the dialogue of mournings, it might be this very fact that will encourage them to find their own solutions to the difficulties they are facing.

As the psychoanalyst Ginette Raimbault observed, the work of writers, artists, poets and musicians is very important to help bring out the universal nature of what a mourner feels, but not in the sense that they will all feel the same thing. On the contrary, 'What no one can understand about my pain, someone can express it in such a way that I can recognize myself in what I cannot share.'

We can find no better example of this dialogue of mournings than in the work of the artist Sophie Calle. Her project *Exquisite Pain* is in one sense a perfect illustration of the work of mourning as described by Freud. Arriving at the Imperial Hotel in New Delhi to meet her lover after a ninety-two-day journey, she receives a telegram informing her that he is in hospital in France. It turns out that his minor ailment is an excuse to break off the relationship, and Calle is left in the bleak hotel room alone with her grief. *Exquisite Pain* consists of ninety-nine different descriptions of what happened that night: the telegram, her call to France, her realization that it had ended, the details of the room. Each description goes over these details in a different way, as if to mimic the Freudian process of accessing the object in all its different representations. Each description is a memory from which the libido must be progressively detached.

But this isn't all. Calle arranges each of her descriptions on the left-hand side of the page. On the right are ninety-nine texts, all giving answers to the question 'When did you suffer most?' posed to both friends and strangers. The beauty of the work lies in this clarification of the mourning process. Each of her own descriptions is in dialogue with the description of someone else. It's as if Calle needs other people's stories to process her own, or even to be able to see her own *as a story*. Towards the end of the series, comments start to emerge in her descriptions, such as 'nothing special', 'not a lot', 'it's the same story' and 'an ordinary story'. The events are losing their libidinal charge, as if the strength of her attachments is being progressively weakened. Now they just appear as any other sad story that she could be hearing about from someone else, like the sweet-shop we discussed earlier that had become just one shop among many.

Calle's project brings to mind the well-known Buddhist story of a woman grieving the death of her first and only child. She wears him strapped to her chest and travels from place to place searching for a treatment to cure him. Eventually a holy man receives her and tells her to bring him some mustard seeds from a house where no one has died. She starts to visit homes, and wherever she goes she ends up listening to stories of death and loss. No house is exempt. As she realizes that she is not alone in her grief, she can at last put her child's body to rest.

Calle's work illustrates the bridge between the private model of mourning described by Freud, in which representations of the lost loved one are run through to the point of exhaustion, and the inter-subjective, public dimension we have been discussing.

But what kind of mechanism is at play here? How exactly does the process work? In some ways it is reminiscent of what Freud termed 'hysterical identification'. This type of identification is different from others in that it doesn't suppose an emotional or erotic tie to the person we identify with. When we looked at the identifications with the dead person that take place after a loss, these are clearly linked to our relationship with the departed. But hysterical identification does not rely on a close bond: all that matters is the idea that we share something with someone else, that we are in or aspire to be in the same situation as them.

Imagine a coughing epidemic at a boarding school. It starts when one girl receives a letter from her lover, perhaps signalling the end of the relationship. Her response is a coughing fit. Soon, all the girls in her class are coughing. But not because they have any particular interest in her as an individual. Rather, they are interested in her relation with the boy, that is, in her situation. They are not attached to her, but to her attachment. Their symptoms indicate that they are in the same situation as she is, both in the sense of having a lover and, perhaps more profoundly, of being disappointed. The coughing forms a bridge between them, resting on the notion of a shared lack, a common unconscious feeling of disappointment.

Perhaps this is how the dialogue of mournings works. Public outcries of grief, indeed, require no connection at all between those mourning and the celebrity or public figure who has died. What they rely on is putting oneself in the same situation as others who have experienced a loss. The relation of the mourner to their loss is mediated through the relation of another mourner to their own loss. In this way, analysts would say, lack becomes an object. We can note how the process of comparison here has not necessarily resulted in new symptoms. The dialogue of mournings has not pushed Calle, for example, into an identification with her interlocuters, but allowed her to process and work through her own pain and distress. If there is a new symptom here, it is perhaps the creation of the work *Exquisite Pain* itself.

—

The unconscious transaction between mourners can illuminate one of the special features of Joan Didion's book *The Year of Magical Thinking*, in which she chronicles her reactions to the death of her husband. Beyond the elegance of the composition and the grace of her style, the book documents a process not just of inner feelings but of the creation of words. It is not just the story of her husband's death but of her search for words to circumscribe it. The book opens with four italicized lines:

> *Life changes fast.*
> *Life changes in the instant.*
> *You sit down to dinner and life as you know it ends.*
> *The question of self-pity.*

Although each of these lines refers to something concrete and is expanded in the book itself, they return again and again at different moments in the text, as if the words were somehow both units of meaning and simply markers for a point of real, unsymbolizable absence. The reader understands that they are not only words with meanings but *words as such*, material elements, things that don't express any sense, rather like nursery rhymes repeated again and again. The fact that they imposed themselves on Didion, rather than being carefully chosen, reinforces this material, brute function of human language. And we can find this creationist emergence of words at many other moments of loss and tragedy.

When the American journalist Vincent Sheean was mourning the death of his beloved friend Mahatma Gandhi, he described two different ways in which words went through his head. One was the 'ordinary way' of words pronounced, 'words sounding in the inner air'. But the other was like 'ticker tape – words visible in the mind', usually but not always unheard. Most of them were from Shakespeare and the Bible, and they were thrown up with an 'agonising suddenness and an effect of unbearable truth each time'. Sitting in the rose-garden not far from where the Mahatma lay, phrases like 'I cried to him from the depths and he answered me' would impose themselves on Sheean with utter clarity although he had made no effort to summon them up.

This strange efflorescence of words is perhaps an attempt to name what is most real, the hole that has opened up in that person's life. Ordinary language with its networks of meaning and conventional codes is not enough: instead, there is an appeal to a different register within language, words without meaning, empty phrases or even insults repeated again and again.

What the examples of Didion and Sheean show so clearly is how these words, rather than being chosen by the writer, *choose them*. They have the quality of forcing themselves on the mourner, as if words were the one barrier separating them from an abyss and so arrive without warning, bypassing the cognitive mechanisms we might suppose govern our usual uses of language.

This emphasis on the materiality of language may strike a chord with our own experiences of loss. We are witnessing how words converge at the point of what is most unbearable for us, and the clarity of this process gives literary testimonies like that of Didion an added power. They don't just tell us what it was like, but actually show how words are functioning, as if to stage this aspect of grief before our very eyes. They show us not just a loss but how something can be created from loss.

In contrast to the examples of Calle and Didion, mourning will often result not in the creation of words, narratives and works of art but in new symptoms in the very stuff of our bodies, as we see in the phenomenon of anniversary reactions. Freud became aware of this when working with his patient Elizabeth von R, described in his *Studies on Hysteria*. 'This lady,' he wrote, 'celebrated annual festivals of remembrance at the period of her various catastrophes, and on these occasions her vivid visual reproduction and expressions of feeling kept to the date precisely.' She would cry intensely on the anniversary of her husband's death, without any conscious awareness of the date in question.

George Pollock reports the case of a young woman whose father had died suddenly when she was thirteen. She described a daily depression which began at 5.30 p.m. when her husband got back from work. The feelings would emerge at the moment she heard the key turning in the lock. In her analysis, she realized that as a child she had excitedly waited for her father's return from work each day. Although she apparently denied his death, her afternoon depressions took the place of a mourning. In another case, a man's depression would appear with greatest intensity on Tuesday afternoons, the day of his mother's death when he was fourteen. Such anniversary reactions are amazingly common, yet most often go unnoticed since the person is unaware of the link themselves and the doctor may not be alert to the unconscious processes at play.

As later analysts investigated these anniversary reactions, they found that they occurred especially in cases of physical illness. Bodily symptoms ranging from the mild to the serious would emerge on the anniversary of an important date, usually one linked to a bereavement or separation. In one of the first large-scale hospital studies in the States, it was found that adult hospitalization dates coincided remarkably with the anniversaries of childhood losses. After his own mother's death, Pollock became fascinated with these forms of unconscious timekeeping. The appearance of anniversary symptoms indicated that the work of mourning had not been successful, so that these punctual, residual phenomena remained.

When the writer Gogol was sixteen, his father became ill and died two years later at the age of forty-three. On hearing the news, he wrote to his mother 'True, at first I was terribly stricken by this news; however, I didn't let anyone know I was saddened. But when I was left alone, I gave myself up to all the power of mad desperation. I even wanted to make an attempt on my own life.' This is exactly what Gogol did more than twenty years later, when he committed suicide through starvation at the age of forty-three. Shortly before he died, he said that his father had died at the same age and 'of the same disease' .

The work of analysts on anniversary reactions is supported by anthropological research. When Geoffrey Gorer was studying the erosion of mourning rituals in industrialized societies, he observed how this absence could have effects in the flesh itself. Physical symptoms in the bereaved were found by many studies to be much more frequent in those geographical regions where mourning rituals were least prevalent. The greater the symbolic, social elaboration of death, the more the mourner's grief would be woven into the community. Physical symptoms and somatizations would occur when mourning was blocked or un-successful.

Anniversary reactions, Pollock showed, would emerge not only when the person reached the age of the deceased, but also when they reached the age of a third party linked to the deceased. Pollock observed that in cases where the father's death occurred before that of the mother, anniversary symptoms often emerged on reaching the age of the mother at the time of the father's death. Also, the person might fall ill at the moment that their own child reached the age they had been when their parent had died or separated from them. This is something we see very often in analytic practice: someone becomes acutely depressed in adult life, yet nothing of any significance seems to have happened to them in the recent past. As we learn more, we discover that the depression has been precipitated by the birthday of one of their children, who has now reached the age which that person was when they had experienced a loss or tragedy in their own childhood.

Such forms of timekeeping are very common, and use not only dates but many other markers to index the past. Whenever the actress Billie Whitelaw heard the popular song 'You are my sunshine', she would be overcome by an inexplicable sadness. The feeling would engulf her but she simply didn't understand why, until, some thirty years later, her mother mentioned that she would cry after her father's death while listening to this record, as it reminded her of his going away. After learning this from her mother, Whitelaw no longer felt her sadness. A connection of memories had taken the place of this anniversary-style reaction.

Pollock saw this as one aim of psychoanalysis: to allow memories to take the place of anniversary reactions. But he also felt that certain losses could never be adequately mourned, such as that of a dead child by a mother. This raises a number of questions about the apparent 'closure' of the process of mourning. The documented prevalence of anniversary symptoms suggests that in fact most bereaved people have not 'got over' their loss. Records from GP surgeries will reveal that many patients return in exactly the same week or month as their previous visit, even if these trips are spaced out over a number of years. Rather than access their memories, the body commemorates them.

———

These problems are often obscured by shallow pictures of the mourning process. Innumerable textbooks tell us what to expect after the experience of a loss. First, a stunned reaction and sense of numbness. Then a denial of the facts, followed by a period of anger. The anger may then metamorphose into a time of magical thinking, when we hope to re-find the loved one. And this may be followed by a depressive spell and then finally a gradual acceptance of the loss. Although these surface descriptions can be informative, they tell us little about the mechanisms involved, and, more significantly, they do not alert us to phenomena like the anniversary reactions we have discussed. In order to understand better the psychology of mourning, we need to move beyond mere descriptions of behaviour and continue to explore the changes in unconscious mental life which may take place in this painful, difficult period.

The first question to ask here is what does a mourning need to accomplish? Should we be prescriptive or just accept that it will be different for different people? The frequency of blocked and arrested mournings means that we cannot shy away from these questions. If mourning so often goes wrong, we are obliged to ask what it would need to go right. Many people remain trapped throughout their lives in mournings that never end. The work of mourning, Freud observes, may seem to actually prolong the existence of the one we have lost. As the mental process of bringing up memories and hopes linked to the one we've lost continues, how does it know when to stop?

If moving through all these details, memories and expectations prolongs the existence of the lost loved one, we might wonder how this can be reconciled with the idea that the process results in a detachment, a distancing. Does something further have to take place? And is there a moment in the process when the existence of the mourned object slides into non-existence? Freud's formulation might seem to imply that there will be a point when all aspects of our attachment will be run through and it will be met with a resounding judgement of non-existence. It suggests that, beyond the actual 'work' of mourning described by Freud, something has to happen *to* this work.

Analytic writers have been divided on this issue: 'Mourning is for life,' said the psychoanalyst Margaret Little, and although a clinician with the acumen of Helene Deutsch could speak of a necessity to mourn, she was later sceptical about any completion of internal processes. Freud, likewise, took care to point out how a loss could never be entirely compensated for. In a 1929 letter to Binswanger, he wrote:

We will never find a substitute [after a loss]. No matter what may fill the gap, even if it be filled completely, it nevertheless remains something else. And actually, this is how it should be, it is the only way of perpetuating that love which we do not want to relinquish.

In Electra's words, 'Never will sorrow forget.'

But why should mourning imply forgetting? After Albert's death, Queen Victoria famously kept her husband's study exactly as it had been when he was alive, prohibiting change of a single detail. Every day, his linens were changed and his clothes laid out, and water prepared for his shaving. We keep mementoes, objects and the possessions of the dead to remind us, not to make us forget. Forgetting, indeed, is often deemed improper. Speaking of the death of her husband, John Maynard Keynes, the Russian dancer Lydia Lopokova said that she had worn his pyjamas for years to keep him close to her. Yet later she could say, 'When he died I suffered a lot. I thought that I could never live without him. Yet now I never think of him.'

The cliché that losses need to be worked through so that we can move beyond them suggests that mourning is something that can be done and dusted. We are encouraged so often to 'get over' a loss, yet bereaved people and those who have experienced tragic losses know full well that it is less a question of getting over a loss and on with life, than finding a way to make that loss a part of one's life. Living with loss is what matters, and writers and artists show us the many different ways in which this can be done. But what are its preconditions? What needs to happen for a mourning to be able to take place?

3

We have emphasized the role of other people in mourning. How someone else has shown their re-action to a loss will be crucial for the way that we, in turn, deal with our own losses. But how far can this unconscious transaction go? If it might get a mourning started in many cases, it is not enough to keep it going: the momentum must have other sources, and a number of things need to happen during a mourning which take place beyond our conscious awareness. This raises some crucial questions: what are the unconscious processes that characterize the work of mourning? And once a mourning gets started, can it ever really end?

Clinicians working with the bereaved and those who have suffered difficult separations have noticed a peculiar phenomenon. A mourning is often punctu-ated by dreams which, unlike others, do not call out for interpretation. They are more like indications of where the mourner is in the process, a kind of mapping of their situation. And among these dreams a special motif frequently emerges: doorways, arches, stages and the many other features that serve to frame a space.

Now, psychoanalysis does not accept that there are any fixed dream-symbols. A snake in one person's dream may evoke the phallus, but in another's may be linked to a childhood scene involving a real snake, just as it may represent someone in that person's circle of family or friends. What an image stands for will depend on the particular history of each individual and the context of each dream. A frame may of course be linked to this particularity, but its appearance in such dreams does indicate something very basic beyond any idea of symbolism: that space is divided up, and that one space now becomes the object of special attention. What can this tell us about mourning?

Freud's account of the process of mourning involves, as we've seen, the idea of an exhaustion of representations. The representations of the lost object are brought again and again into painful focus and the memories and hopes linked to it met by the judgement that the object no longer exists. As this process continues, so the work of mourning will gradually exhaust itself. But how might such a process be distinguished from one in which the subject remains haunted by representations? What, after all, is to stop the piecemeal process described by Freud from continuing for ever? At what point does the cycle exhaust itself, if at all? This is where the motif of the frame becomes especially interesting.

A frame divides up space. And, in a very precise sense, it draws attention to whatever lies within its boundaries. Imagine watching a sunset and enjoying its beauty. Now, imagine that we put a frame around the image of the sunset. This will remind us that what we're looking at is an image, a representation, perhaps one that culture has taught us to see as beautiful. We might have been lost in the beauty of the scene, but the frame is saying, 'This is a representation; it is con-ditioned.' In other words, a frame draws attention to the artificial nature of what we see.

Eighteenth-century humorists made much of this type of conditioning, poking fun at how the public was being taught to see certain outdoor scenes as 'nature'. Jane Austen evokes this artificiality slyly in *Northanger Abbey*, when we learn that Catherine Morland has dismissed her view of the city of Bath from Beechen Cliff as 'unworthy to make part of a landscape'. The very idea of 'landscape' was forged by culture, not nature. When we become aware of this kind of framing, the image has been shifted to another level: it now inhabits a different space, the space of signs, a representational space. It is no longer simply an object – the sunset – but the representation of that object. It is situated in another register.

We can see this in the very particular ways that Renaissance portraits introduce frames. Many of them include a frame within the picture itself, using stone columns or the wall of a balcony as in the 'Mona Lisa', or creating one in the form of the actual background scenery. The Russian critic Boris Uspensky drew attention to the way that frames and backgrounds have the same function here: they indicate that what we see takes place on an artificial stage, in a symbolic as opposed to a real space. The backgrounds would be painted according to an artistic system which differed from that used in the rest of the painting. Whereas the main figure would be painted using certain codes of size and scale, the background would depict landscape using an alternative system, often one that could not be found in the real world. Mountains, castles and other features would be situated in an impossible space, clashing with the realism and detail of the human figure. The same logic of contrasts could apply to the introduction of stock stereotypical characters in drama: they signify a symbolic, unreal element by emphasizing their own conventionality. The increased convention-ality of a stage set or a character or a frame or a back-ground embodies, as it were, frames within the frame, showing us how we are in a different space. They draw our attention to the register of artificiality.

Doesn't this provide a clue to understanding what needs to happen to stop the mourning process going on for ever? In Freud's account, after all, what is there to indicate that we are no longer haunted by the one we've lost? The Austrian psychoanalyst Franz Kalten-beck has suggested that perhaps all the representations of the lost object must be gathered up into a set: they must pass from being representations to another level. This transformation implies that the representations must be framed: they must be represented *as represent-ations*. It is no longer a question of the image we think we see in the street, the tone of voice we think we hear in a crowded room, the presence we expect momentarily when the phone or the doorbell rings. Rather, we come to give certain representations the value of representing all these others.

In the famous example, Marcel Proust's taste of a madeleine dipped in tea or sight of a cracked paving-stone in Venice acted as conduits for overpowering sequences of feelings, ideas and emotions linked to a lost love. The little details that Proust made so much of had become symbolic of memory and loss, but what would happen if everything in one's reality had this status, if every paving-stone were a cracked one? As one melancholic man put it, he was terrified lest 'the past return at any moment', assailing him 'as a state of mind or even body and carry with it grief, fear and hopeless rage'.

Being at the mercy of the past so completely is unbearable, and so, if the work of mourning is to take place, certain precise details must be selected, conferring on them an elective power: they become symbols, representing other chains of thoughts and feelings, standing in for them or taking their place. This indicates a change of levels: it's the difference between being haunted by every aspect of reality and having found ways of representing that reality, emptying it out, transforming it: turning it, as it were, into a representation. As the same melancholic man put it, 'I want to put the past in the past, but not to forget it. I just don't want to be seized by the past.'

The British psychoanalyst Ella Sharpe noticed something similar in her clinical work. She observed how it was always a significant moment when a patient suffering from a particular problem became able to represent this problem as somehow separate from themselves. A drug addict or a fetishist, for example, could talk about their symptom for ages, but the moment that this symptom appeared as an element in their dreams, its status had changed. It was no longer simply a representation, a motif in their everyday talk, but had now changed levels: there was a new focus on its quality *as a representation*. In our terms, it had passed from being a representation to being a representation of a representation.

A frame, in the sense of a border, a window or an arch, for example, allows what is seen to be situated as a representation. And this is echoed by the ubiquity in the dreams of bereaved people of the motif of a stage. This again focuses attention on the artificiality of what is being played out, its quality not as a natural scene but as a representation. This accent on the symbolic, artificial character of an action or scene so often marks a point of progress in the long and difficult process of mourning. Like the sunset's transformation into the framed sunset, it shows that another level of symbolization has been reached, a different space. The loss is now being inscribed in a symbolic space.

Mourning thus involves a certain *making artificial*. Isn't this, indeed, the very principle behind the idea of the monument? When some terrible tragedy takes place, it hardly ever happens that the site itself is just left untouched. The houses where Jeffrey Dahmer or the Wests carried out their murders, for example, are not left to act as memorials. Rather, in order to become memorials, they have to be changed: either through total demolition and then erection of a new structure, or through some alteration or intervention. What matters is the fact that something artificial take place, some act that will mark the space. This making artificial is perhaps the simplest form of what a monument is. The space cannot be allowed to remain the same as it was before the moment of tragedy and loss.

This emphasis on the artificial can perhaps solve a puzzle that has long perplexed anthropologists and historians. Many cultures have mourning rituals which involve the reversal of established conventions. Men, for example, will have to dress as women and vice versa, or the order of dishes served in a feast will be inverted, or social hierarchies temporarily reversed so that slaves become masters. These diverse practices have generated all sorts of interpretations, usually attempting to find symbolism in the changes. The man dressing as a woman means he is feminized, the worker becoming master for a day implies a wish-fulfilment, the inverted order at the feast signifies that the world has been turned upside down by a death. While some of these explanations may have value, aren't they missing something very fundamental? Aren't they missing exactly what is brought into focus by the idea of the frame?

By reversing established conventions, these practices illuminate the symbolic, artificial nature of social reality. Gender roles, social hierarchies and eating customs can all be inverted precisely because they are symbolic conventions. What this aspect of mourning ritual does is draw attention *to the symbolic dimension*. This has been deeply affected by the disappearance of a member of the group, so now the whole of the group's customs and conventions must be shown to be disturbed. In some rituals, after relating the life of the deceased, the lives of all their relations are recounted, then those of the ancestors, allies, and then, by extension, the whole history of the village and neighbouring villages. The death is thus integrated into not just the local history of the next of kin but the entire symbolic world of the community.

Beyond the meaning of individual practices here, the shifts show a mobilization of the socio-symbolic structure itself in response to the hole opened up by the loss. After a death, it is not only the deceased him or herself who is altered, but words, food, housing and all a community's activities may become subject to prohibitions and changes. Everything is affected, just as Melanie Klein had sensed when she spoke of the necessity to re-create *the whole* of one's internal world with each loss. But where Klein had seen this as a sign that the *internal* world had to be re-created, it is in fact the entire *symbolic* world of convention that must be refashioned.

This emphasis on the symbolic is illuminated by the artist Thomas Demand, who takes photographs of scenes he has reconstructed through meticulous, life-size cardboard models. Demand will often choose a site linked to loss and grief, some trauma or moment of missed opportunity that cannot be readily symbolized, and then rebuild it anew in a completely artificial way before photographing it. His subjects range from the Stasi headquarters, a corridor leading to Jeffrey Dahmer's apartment, to the bunker where a failed attempt to assassinate Hitler took place. Critics of Demand's work complain that this exercise is pointless: why couldn't he just have photographed the original space? On immediate viewing, after all, they look identical to their sources. This is to miss the crucial point: confronted with the unsymbolizable nature of the crime or tragedy, the symbolic dimension itself has to be mobilized, and hence the emphasis will be on the register of the artificial, following the same principle as the reversals found in tribal rituals. Demand is showing us how the artificial has a vital function. Even if the space looks the same, it isn't, because it has been artificially created.

It is interesting to note here how, much to the displeasure of those anthropologists who wish to find an ideal of nature in the peoples they study, mourning and burial rituals, even while adhered to, are frequently complained about by the participants themselves. 'It's all so artificial, so pointless', the inhabitants of a remote village might grumble. Where the Western eye wishes to find a community totally at peace with itself, functioning seamlessly with none of the alienation present in our own culture, the facts belie this. Instead, we find the same accent on the artificial that, despite being troubling for those involved, is necessary for mourning to operate. Even in Victorian times, when the outward display of mourning was so essential, there was no shortage of mockery of the rituals involved and the chains of shops specializing in the latest mourning garb were the subject of perpetual lampoon.

This emphasis on the artificial finds a further echo in the way we start to use language. Like cultural customs relating to eating habits, gender and social roles, language itself is governed by convention. Words do not have a natural, essential link to what they refer to, but we learn to use them according to patterns of convention. It is a significant moment in language learning when children register this basic fact: that there is an arbitrary relation between words and things. Children, perhaps, move properly into language not when they use words to name things, but when words start to lose their connection to things and the context of their first use.

Pointing to the crescent-shaped object in the sky and saying 'moon' doesn't indicate that a child can speak, and nor does pointing to a grapefruit segment on one's plate and using the same word. Rather, speech is functioning when the child can then displace its use to other less related contexts. Words are functioning autonomously, further and further away from their original referents. This means that the symbolic, artificial dimension of language is established not when the child points to the dog and says 'Woof', but when he says 'Woof' pointing to the cat. This indicates entry into a new, symbolic space. The child has understood that it is convention that governs the use of words.

This is exactly what we see in childhood phobias. A dog or a horse suddenly becomes an object of fear, and as its genesis is traced it turns out that the animal comes not from the 'natural' environment of the child but from the artificial world of story-books. In other words, they have chosen an animal rich in symbolic density. These animals then start to do things that no real animal can do: they dispense justice, they make threats, they scold and even sometimes reward. By constantly changing their function, they become distanced from real animals and become privileged as signs, cut off from their original referents. No real dog or horse could do what these phobic creations now do. And often the child will make sure that the artificial nature of these creatures is conveyed. After drawing a giraffe, the phobic five-year-old boy Little Hans discussed by Freud crumpled it up and announced the new beast as 'crumpled giraffe'. Found in no nature reserve, 'crumpled giraffe' could only be created by symbolic conventions, by words, and Hans's production emphasizes precisely this symbolic, artificial dimension.

Why should such symbolic entities appear in phobia? Hans was confronted with a problem situation. A little sister had been born and he had started to experience his first erections. These elements threw his world into disarray, and his phobia was an attempt to refigure it, to reorganize everything. The horse he was afraid of was like the Superhero who arrives at the crucial moment to save ordinary mortals from crime or menace. But it helped Hans not by removing his enemies, but by re-ordering his everyday world. Fear of the horse would determine where he was allowed to go or not go, what he was allowed to do or not do. As his phobia developed, every element of his world became linked to it in one way or another.

There is a curious echo of the work of mourning here. Just as a serious phobia will gradually involve every aspect of one's reality, so mourning moves through all the constituents of one's world. Phobia involves the work of reshuffling elements, to situate a new symbolic configuration which responds to the emergence of something difficult to process. What we see here is a very basic mechanism that is set in motion when we experience a loss. There is an appeal to the symbolic dimension to resolve the situation. Hence the accent on artificiality and representation that we have noted in both mourning rites and phobia. Just as in a phobia we will see an accentuation of the properties of a representation *as a representation* (Little Hans's crumpled giraffe), so we will see in mourning an emphasis or enhancement of the semiotic qualities of a representation (the frame, the stage). This signals a shift from the representation of a so-called reality (that of the loved object) to a representation of a representation of that reality. It now inhabits a symbolic space.

This is exactly what we find in the section of Freud's *Interpretation of Dreams* where he deals with absurdity and contradiction. Why, Freud asks, do some dreams seem completely absurd, bypassing all norms of sense and meaningfulness? Such dreams involve a combination of elements or situations that could never be found together in reality. They create nothing less than artificial hybrids, but rather than simply seeking a hidden symbolism here beneath these strange inventions, why not see them as emblems of artificiality itself? By pointing to their own artificiality, they show us that something cannot be thought through or symbolized. And it is surely significant that nearly all of the examples that Freud gives of absurd dreams take place in the context of bereavement and death. The most famous of them concerns a dead father who does not know that he is dead. The impossibility of processing the father's death is transformed into the absurdity of the dream's premise.

We see something of this impossibility of thinking through and symbolizing in many forms of artistic creation. To take a recent example, the Turkish artist Kutlug Ataman is well known for his interest in the stories of everyday people in marginal or excluded communities. In 'Twelve', a work shown at the Tate, he films six members of a small village in south-east Turkey talking about their lives and their belief in reincarnation. The detail of these histories allows us to enter this closed, alien world. But in 'Kuba', an installation made for Art Angel in London, the work consists of an installation of around 100 video monitors, each one playing a long filmed interview with the different members of a shanty-town community. As we become drawn in to the individual stories and narratives, we realize the impossibility of taking them all in. They cannot be entirely encompassed, except in a fragmentary way, one by one. While the work is about the representations of the particular, unique life of each of the interviewees, it is also about how they have been gathered up into a set, and it is this very act which confers a sense of impossibility. They simply cannot be taken in, digested, encompassed all at once. And yet, at the same time, the work itself is just this: the collection of all their stories.

We see a similar process in the work of W. G. Sebald, which has been described by one psychiatrist as an 'anti anti-depressant'. Sebald's books focus on apparently random, contingent details, such as an old photograph he finds or a stone wall he comes across, and he then starts to explore their history. As he does so, choosing tiny rather than mighty historical figures as his guides, he brings into focus not simply the individual life behind the photo or the stone wall but, more fundamentally, the impossibility of encompassing all the lives behind all those details that make up human culture.

If one stone wall can lead to a real story of loss and absence, imagine what would happen if we began to think about every stone wall in the same way. Human civilization would then become an immense hole, an abyss that Sebald's writing evokes for us. It is exactly this unthinkable hole that his work circumscribes.

—

The second element which shows that a mourning process is under way is also found in dreams. It often happens that a mourner dreams of killing the very person whose death they are bewailing. This can be terrifying and confusing for the dreamer. Why on earth would they dream of murdering the one they love? The panic this causes sometimes even spurs them to seek out an analyst or therapist. What is being represented here? Is it a repressed wish of the dreamer? Or something else?

In the film *Marathon Man*, Dustin Hoffman plays a young history graduate caught up in a Nazi plot to smuggle diamonds many years after the Second World War. Laurence Olivier plays the fiendish dentist who tortures him to find out whether it is safe to collect the jewels from a safe deposit box. During the course of this we learn that Hoffman's father had been a victim of the McCarthy anti-communist witch-hunts and had taken his own life. In his desk drawer Hoffman keeps the gun which the father had used to shoot himself, and the viewer is continually reminded that the son has not been able to mourn his dead father properly.

After the final scene in which Hoffman and Olivier do battle, the Nazi dentist is killed and it is only at this point that Hoffman can take his father's gun and throw it away. The sequence suggests that it is only once he has killed the father, embodied by the ageing Olivier, that he can actually start to detach himself from the ghost of his own father. In a sense, he has killed the dead in order to allow a true mourning to begin.

Freud thought that the work of mourning involved a declaration that the lost object is dead. In a letter to Ernest Jones, he noted that the work of mourning involves 'bringing the recognition of the reality principle to every point of the libido ... one then has the choice of dying oneself or of acknowledging the death of the loved one, which again comes very close to your expression that one kills this person ...' Where Klein believed that mourning was about demonstrating that we have *not* killed the dead, for Freud it is precisely the symbolic killing of the dead that will allow a mourning to take place.

But why the necessity of killing the dead? If we take Freud seriously – that we always reproach the one we've lost for departing – we might have a very good reason for wishing them dead. Our rage at them will take the form of a death-wish which demands representation. We need to let this be voiced before we can temper our relation to the dead. But is this really the most convincing explanation?

Mourning is about much more than real biological death. It is also about laying someone to rest symbolically. When someone dies, we often behave as if they are not entirely dead. We talk in whispers around a coffin, and are careful not to malign the dead with malevolent or disrespectful remarks. The burial rites studied by anthropologists show the same precaution: every measure must be taken to ensure that the dead don't return to take vengeance on us. Heavy coffin lids or stones tied to the body, the breaking of leg bones to keep them immobile, charms and amulets to deter their attacks, and a whole range of sacrifices and tokens have this palliative, protective function.

Precious objects are often buried with the dead to make sure they are kept happy and distracted, and the custom of binding the limbs of cadavers, once understood as a sign of ritual murder, is now seen as a measure most probably taken to ensure that they don't return. Burying possessions is less a mark of devotion and respect than a warding-off. Many cultures require that the body of the deceased does not leave the house it died in through the main door, as this would allow it to return. It must leave through a specially built hole in the wall, which is then swiftly resealed. In some rites, mourners run in a zigzag pattern away from the grave so as to dodge the ghost of the departed. Anecdotal evidence has it that some indigenous cultures saw the arrival of white men as the return of the dead, because they seemed so eager to kill people and cause harm.

At the same time, our culture is full of stories, books and films about the dead never quite dying, from the ever-popular cycle of zombie movies to the endless tales of ghouls and vampires. This animism ascribed to the dead is yet one more sign that at some level we believe that the dead are always just about to come back. To stop this, the undead need to die, and besides the figure of the greedy blood-sucking vampire it is significant that we also find the sad, world-weary vampire who longs to be properly put to rest.

Killing the dead is central to many other aspects of popular culture. Is there a single major Hollywood film nowadays in which the villain only dies once? Even if the story has nothing to do with horror or science fiction genres, today's bad guys will invariably get shot, stabbed, burned, drowned or thrown from some great height, yet this first 'death' does not kill them. They always come back a bit later to threaten the hero and so have to be dispatched a second time. Rather than seeing this as a cheap ploy to excite suspense, why not recognize the basic mechanism of laying to rest: for the living to feel safe and secure, the dead have to die twice.

Real biological death is thus different from proper, symbolic death. The anthropologist Robert Hertz documented the discrepancy here between mourning and burial rites. Many peoples employ rituals which address this separation, having a second burial ceremony when it is judged that the deceased has reached their true destination and is finally at rest. Greek tragedy is full of references to the fact that biological and symbolic death do not always coincide. For symbolic death to occur, the dead must be banished and kept at bay. They must take up a place in the world of their ancestors, or, in a more general sense, in the world of the dead. Some peoples will draw a circle around the dead to contain them, and implore ancestors to accept them, to keep them there.

The dead become relocated and assigned a new role and function within the social group.

We find the same split in the Christian tradition. A major problem for Reformation thinkers was the question of what happens between death and the Last Judgement. Is the soul awake and active in this time or asleep? What kind of life was there between these two poles? Might the soul even cease to exist as an independent entity after the death of the body? These debates show how biological death and laying to rest are never the same thing. The standard idea that the soul leaves the body at death to reside in the spiritual realms of heaven, hell or purgatory where it will await the Last Judgement proved intolerable to many thinkers as it left so many unanswered questions. What was asleep and what was really dead? Was there a difference between extinction and a temporal pause in existence? Could the soul experience a syncope?

These tortuous dilemmas illuminate the mourner's dreams of killing the dead. They indicate that the dead have now died a second time: that they are, as it were, dead again. The second killing represents a movement from empirical biological death to symbolic laying to rest. And that would explain why these dreams tend to be a positive sign in the mourning process.

—

The distinction between real and symbolic death is perhaps confused for us today by the fact that so often the order seems reversed. Rather than biological death preceding symbolic death, it is as if the symbolic death comes first. Deathbed scenes used to take place in homes and in the community, but today they increasingly take place in hospitals. The chances of someone dying in their community today are less than one in five. Isolated from their usual infrastructure and kept alive by a variety of technological and pharmaceutical means, the sick person dies symbolically before their body actually gives up the ghost.

Once they are dead biologically, on the other hand, rather than a laying to rest symbolically, there is an ever-increasing effort to keep the dead with us. Immediate destruction of the dead person's possessions would seem odd in our culture, but not in many others, where it is widely practised. Whereas in some cultures all the objects and mementoes of the dead person are destroyed, in ours we have a habit of keeping them. It is as if by letting go of the objects, we are letting go of our memories of the person. Even the images and voices of the dead are retained. New internet remembrance sites offer a kind of live memorial, where we can see and hear the deceased. TV shows commemorate dead celebrities, and a vast industry of remembering has emerged in our time. There is less of an idea today that a line must be drawn between the living and the dead, and we are encouraged to maintain a closeness to the departed.

This might seem like a good thing. We have seen already how catastrophic it can be if a loss goes unmourned and unrepresented. At the same time, however, it is worth thinking about the kind of closeness we are encouraged to pursue. This is reflected in the mass of false information and myths about how other societies mourn. We are often told how, in

African or Asian cultures, the dead are continually among the living. It is only in the West, we are told, that the dead are forgotten. But this is largely untrue. A shared characteristic of many of the non-Western mourning rites we have discussed is precisely their effort to banish the dead. They are no longer to dwell among the living, but must be kept at a distance. Alterity with the dead replaces continuity.

On the other hand, the dead are not forgotten in these cultures, since the social group registers their disappearance. The rituals inscribe loss within a community, and no longer as an individual experience. Funeral rites have this function: to turn the dead, restless being into a proper ancestor. As anthropologists have observed, the whole presence of ritual is there to demonstrate that the dead do not *automatically* become ancestors. After mourning and burial rites, social structures change, and formal rules govern the relation of the new set of ancestors to their descendants. The key is that the dead are installed in the ancestral line. Their rights and duties are redistributed. Functions are reallocated. Filiation matters here rather than continuity. The dead are not present via communication with the living, but by a reordering of the social group.

This reordering always involves a separation of the immediate, everyday world and the symbolic, artificial space that we have discussed: it's the difference between the giraffe drawn by Little Hans and the 'crumpled giraffe' he produces next. And it is also, we have argued, why so many mourning rituals include inversions of conventional social practices. As Lisa Appignanesi writes, it is only by remembering the dead that we can lose them properly, and this remembering implies a symbolic reordering of one's world. When Westerners speak casually about the childish belief in ghosts and communication with the dead in indigenous cultures, they are in fact talking about *their own* culture. It is us and not them who cannot separate from the dead.

—

Killing the dead is an essential aspect of mourning. But what about the death-wishes that we all harbour towards the living – especially the ones we love the most? Freud's younger brother died at eight months when Freud was nearly two years old, and he wrote to his friend Wilhelm Fliess that this loss had fulfilled the death-wishes he had had against his rival, arousing self-reproaches, a tendency which had remained with him ever since. As we grow up, frustrations and disappointments inevitably produce death-wishes which are vigorously pushed out of consciousness. These form part of our unconscious mental life, emerging in slips of the tongue, symptoms or dreams. When someone we love dies, wouldn't this mean that at some level we will feel responsible? We wished for their death in the past and now it has happened. It's as if they have died *because* of our wishes.

This difficult strand of our mental life forms another thread in the knot of killing the dead. Perhaps we need to represent these wishes in order to become less tangled up in them and the guilt they generate. Once we have seen ourselves killing the dead – staged the murder, as it were – it is then easier to mourn them.

We have accepted, at some level, our ambivalence. The problem, of course, is when our guilt is too strong. We can become overpowered by feelings of guilt at the death, although often this will be experienced consciously as anxiety or fatigue, not as the direct sensation of guilt.

Such Freudian ideas might seem far-fetched to our conscious minds, but cultural rituals show how seriously they are taken. Death-wishes tend to be treated in roughly two ways: there are the 'comedies of innocence' in which guilt is shifted as far away as possible from the initial person, and then there are the rituals of punishment in which they are judged guilty whatever their actual situation. The best example of a 'comedy of innocence' is the Bouphonia, practised in classical Greece in honour of Zeus. A line of oxen is driven round an altar on which grain has been laid. The first animal to start munching is slain with an axe, and the slayer then flees while the ox is butchered and eaten. A trial ensues, in which the water-carriers whose water had cleaned the axe blame those who sharpened it; they in turn blame the man who handed over the axe; he blames the butcher; the butcher blames the knife used to cut up the body, and the knife, unable to defend itself, is thrown into the sea. The ox-hide is then stuffed, raised up and yoked to a plough. Through this resurrection, the murder is symbolically annulled.

Guilt for a murderous act is doubly displaced here, not only through the shift of blame in the trial but through the apparently 'guilty' act of the first ox in eating the grain. This tries to remove guilt by putting an arbitrary, unpredictable act at the origin of the whole process, a kind of alibi or smoke-screen for the guilty act of the ox-murderer that will follow. We can find a similar logic in the world of modern fiction. Think, for example, of the novels of Patricia Highsmith. She describes again and again a situation in which a certain character wishes to murder someone. They brood for months or years, they plot and plan with the utmost precision and industry. And then, just as they are about to commit the act, some random accident occurs which finishes off the intended victim: a brick falls on their head, they fall over or someone else kills them. In Highsmith's universe, the motive and the act can't be in the same place at the same time: death-wish and murder are kept apart via the intervention of contingent factors that have little to do with the narrative.

This impossibility of assuming one's death-wishes is inverted in those cultural rituals in which guilt is assumed from the start. When someone dies, there is an automatic series of punishments levied on the surviving kin, as if they had to be reprimanded for their part in the death. Some African societies, for example, will inflict violence on a mourner, insulting them, beating them and humiliating them. This seems to externalize the feelings of guilt. When a loved one dies, the mourner is treated as guilty without any trial. The community behaves as if that person is guilty, so pre-empting their entanglement in their own unconscious guilt. The social group punishes mourners before they have the chance to punish themselves.

These forces are so powerful that many cultures

have strict injunctions forbidding mourners to harm themselves. Better to be punished by the group than to punish oneself. The Old Testament contains prohibitions on self-laceration, Hellenistic laws were enforced to prevent women reproducing on their own bodies the wounds found on the corpses of their loved ones, and even today countless cultures witness self-cutting, beating, berating and pain-inflicting after a death. By making the group fulfil this function, mourners are protected from themselves, and their grief is inscribed instead into the social structure. Crucially, the mourner is recognized as guilty.

An ethnologist doing fieldwork in Kenya was studying mourning processes in a village when she had to send her two children on the long journey back to Dakar to join their father. As she saw them off on the bus, the women of the village grouped together and began to hurl insults at her. How could she? What kind of mother was she? What sort of monster would abandon her children? After hours of this chastisement, the ethnologist was reduced to tears and, unable to take any more, exploded in anger at the assembled women. Immediately, they began to laugh uproariously, telling her she'd done the right thing by sending them off. The insults, it seems, were aimed to protect her from her own self-reproaches.

This play between internalization and externalization is crucial for the mourning process. At the memorial service for Monty Python actor Graham Chapman, the mourners had gathered to listen to the usual collection of sober and grief-ridden speeches. When John Cleese took his turn to speak, he began with a solemn opening, before describing his lost friend as a freeloading bastard, followed by a string of further insults. The ensuing laughter was so loud it was difficult to hear the rest of the speech: everyone was in hysterics. He had voiced the fury at Chapman's untimely departure latent in all those who had loved him.

Killing the dead is a way of loosening one's bonds to them and situating them in a different, symbolic space. It may then become possible to start to forge new ties to the living, but this will always follow a course specific to each individual. Family and friends may put pressure on the mourner to go out and meet someone new, but the individual time to mourn must be respected. A problem, however, occurs when a pervasive sense of loyalty to the dead prevents any expression of ties to the living.

This loyalty may be rooted in the guilt feelings that we discussed earlier. Our unconscious hatred is reversed into an overpowering sense of owing something to the dead. Terrible procrastination can surround how much money to spend on a coffin or burial service, which is not made more pleasant by the fact that funerals are always more expensive if planned in advance by the future deceased. In Switzerland, this problem is overcome since it is the state that pays. Small details of a burial, however, can always be recruited in the service of these feelings, as if the basic ambivalence towards the lost loved one were being displaced on to practical issues of the choice of the casket, flowers or refreshments. And this brings us to a crucial question, which we see clinically time and time again: it will become a terrible weight for the mourner when *different dimensions of loyalty* become confused. Loyalty always implies a certain sense of debt, but our relation to a debt can be varied. It is especially complicated after a loss, since it is such a widespread belief that we must give to the dead.

But what are we paying for? There are two forms of debt: the ones that can be repaid, linked to the scales of justice, and the ones that can't. We can owe someone something and pay it back. But we cannot repay the fact, for example, that we have been brought into the world or that our life has been saved. One debt opens up to a whole series of balances and equivalences, the other has something absolute about it, defying quantification.

There is a terrible problem in mourning when *these two dimensions of debt are confused*. If the line between the two debts is blurred, the mourner will find him- or herself in a dreadful situation. How can they pay back an unpayable debt? In one case, a man tortured himself over the question of how he could repay the man who had fathered him, to the extent of tearing at his own body in despair for years after the latter's death. He would pull out his own hair and strike himself. His mother had been a moneylender, and had never tired of pointing out to him how every meal, every bus ticket, every schoolbook she bought for him put him in her debt. For her, it was as if her son's very existence were logged in an account book and would have to be reimbursed. The terrible sense of debt fostered by the mother had come to engulf his relation to his dead father, a loving man who had never once tried to make his son feel guilty for existing.

Confusing these two dimensions of debt is enough to establish a severe disturbance to the mourning process: what is often called a pathological mourning. The person feels that they can neither pay nor leave the debt unpaid. In some cases, where we have the opportunity to speak with someone after a suicide attempt that failed, we are told that the act seemed the only way to escape the dreadful sense of a claim being made on them. In other cases, the confusion takes the form of endless doubt about how much money to spend on the funeral. Sometimes the clinician can intervene effectively here by emphatically acknowledging the symbolic, non-reversible side to a subject's debt.

Telling a patient that they have paid enough or that they should renounce trying to pay an unpayable debt may be well intentioned, but in some cases it can precipitate a further suicide attempt, to show the clinician that the debt cannot be eradicated. Hence the importance, at times, of recognizing that a debt exists and that it cannot be paid. Voicing this sense of debt and articulating it must be separated from the idea of paying it.

These feelings of debt and the confusion they generate can be exacerbated if the dead themselves seem to demand repayment. Many cultures stigmatize certain ways of dying as improper. The dead were not meant to die. Children born in some African societies after a death have conjugatory names like 'No Hope', 'Hole' and 'No One Wants Him' to feign disinterest, to better protect them from the claims of the dead who demand satisfaction. Likewise, a child may have to change their name when a parent dies to stop them from being recognized when the ghost returns to carry them off.

The historian Jean-Claude Schmitt showed in his book about ghosts in the Middle Ages how they would always return to plead for masses, almsgiving or prayer so as to improve their situation in the hereafter. They needed to be released and laid to rest symbolically, but the circumstances of their death prevented this. Failure of suffrages, not having carried out penance before dying, or, later, the non-baptism of a child would result in these states of suspension. If the usual rites of mourning had not been completed, the dead would suffer and make themselves visible to the living. Given this context, they would appear at different times, linked to liturgical details, date of death, and the calendar of feast days. People in the Middle Ages, perhaps, were more alert to anniversary reactions than we are today. When things went wrong, they would look to their calendars in a way that perhaps only the superstitious do today.

The dead here always wanted something from the living. Interestingly, medieval religious texts gave exactly the same advice to those burdened by ghosts as do today's psychotherapists. When the terrifying apparition would make its entrance, the deceased's family were advised to ask it what it wanted. Since ghosts were always ghosts *for a reason* – with something left unpaid or some spiritual debt left in the balance – the only way to get rid of them properly would be to find out what exactly the problem was and then try to solve it. Today, when a child complains of nocturnal visitations by ghosts and ghouls, the psychologically minded clinician might well do the same thing. Often, the child is quite surprised to be asked what they think the ghost wants, and this question can be useful in changing the way that he or she pictures the situation.

—

The third element of mourning concerns its object. This might seem obvious: we mourn the one we have lost. But neither Freud nor Klein nor Lacan saw this as a given. Freud observed in *Mourning and Melancholia* that there may be a difference between whom we have lost and what we have lost in them. This beautiful and sensitive differentiation suggests that perhaps mourning can only progress precisely when we have been able to separate out these two dimensions for ourselves.

Take the controversy over mourning in childhood. Can a two-year-old who loses a parent be said to mourn the loss? It has often been observed that young children who have lost a parent might continue with their everyday activities, with no weeping or withdrawal into preoccupation. It has also struck many researchers how these children sometimes seemed to be in very good moods. Feeling good, after all, is the affective version of denial: if we don't feel bad, then nothing bad has happened. Only much later, in their teens or twenties, would grief hit them, yet usually without any conscious connection with the original loss. A romantic break-up or another death within their circle of friends or family would ignite the grief that had been blocked in childhood. Such processes, which have been well documented, pose the question of whether a young child is able to mourn in the way that an adult does.

Some researchers believe that children cannot mourn, since they have not yet acquired a true concept of death, yet we could ask whether adults have been any more successful. Similarly, we can certainly find many bereaved adults who show no signs of grief or mourning. After a loss, they continue with their lives as if not much has happened; they show up at work as usual, they continue with their hobbies and interests, and avoid speaking about what has taken place. If children cannot mourn, would these adults just be children who have never grown up? Or do they share some defence mechanism or deficit which we could define and explain?

Opinions about childhood mourning remain divided. Some say that mourning does indeed take place, pointing out that we may not notice the subtle ways in which children mourn. Others argue that at such a young age the child will not have formed an adequate idea of the lost loved one to allow true grief. They can't be said to mourn an object until they actually have an idea of what an object – or a person – is. This rather simple point suggests that perhaps mourning is only possible once we have been able to constitute for ourselves an idea of what an object – or a person – is. It is less a question of having an adequate view of death than of having an adequate view of a person: and this, perhaps, already includes within it a conception of loss.

This might explain the once popular idea that mourning can only take place after adolescence. Although clinically this is incorrect, the logic behind it is illuminating. Adolescence, we are told, is the time when we mourn our parents: we give up our attachments to them. This painful time is like a 'trial mourning', an initiation into the process of dealing with loss. When we later on experience a loss through separation or bereavement, we can relate it to what we went through in adolescence. The interest of this idea is that it suggests that one loss must be put in relation to another, earlier loss. *We can only mourn if we have already lost something.*

This is exactly the point made by both Klein and Lacan. Lacan remarked that mourning involves a process of what he calls 'a constitution of the object'. This might seem surprising since we would expect that mourning involves just the opposite: a realization that the object is no more. But Lacan thought that mourning involved the very constitution of the object. And as the psychoanalyst Jean Allouch has pointed out, this idea of the 'constitution' of the object echoes Klein's formula that 'Not until the object is loved as a whole can its loss be felt as a whole.'

What do these formulas mean? And what link do they have to the reality of situations of mourning? To have a notion of the object as a whole has seemed to some theorists to indicate that we have grasped the constancy of our object: we have a stable sense of another person, who remains identical despite being here one moment and absent the next. Klein had a more detailed idea. For her, we begin life with differing relations to what we take to be the good and bad aspects of our surroundings: there is a frustrating breast and a satisfying breast, rather than one breast which at times satisfies and at times frustrates. We will have developed a true sense of an object when we realize that these previously split attributes in fact qualify one and the same object: the breast is both frustrating and gratifying.

Lacan's idea is a bit different. For him, constituting an object means having registered psychically an empty space, the fact that the object we yearn for is definitively lost. We internalize not just the parent but the parent's absence. More precisely, we internalize the empty place of certain objects linked to the parent, such as the breast that we have given up. The objects that we find interesting and attractive in our lives – lovers, friends – all go into this fundamental empty space, and that is what gives them their appeal. Constituting an object means separating the images of those things that matter to us from the *place* that they occupy. Klein and Lacan thus share the idea that for mourning to operate, the object – and the object's place – has to be built up, and that this construction is never a given.

However strange this idea might seem, doesn't it respond to the clinical fact that so often a mourner will return to all their earlier losses before being able to start the work of mourning the one they have lost most recently? For this process to operate, the mourner has to be able to differentiate, at an unconscious level, between the object and the place of an object. And this would presumably bring into focus why they had loved the one they have lost. If the difference between the one we love and the place they have occupied for us can be articulated, then it will be possible to move on to make new investments – to put others into that same empty place.

To map out this difference will mean exploring in detail the reasons why we had become attached to those we love. Mourning a dead or even a divorced spouse, for example, might mean excavating the many links which we had unconsciously made between them and one of our own parents. What features did they have in common? How were they different? What were the pathways which led to our attachment? This process also involves questioning our images of our parents, changing perspectives as well as confronting what was most consistent, most real about them. Through this long and arduous work, the image of the lost loved one can be separated from the place it held for us in the unconscious.

This separation is not just about disentangling our partners, say, from the image of our parents. It is also, as we have emphasized, about separating the image of our parents from the fundamental empty space inscribed in our unconscious, which neither the parents nor anyone else can ever fill or eradicate. This will mean a recognition of the fundamental alterity or otherness of the one we've loved: as their image is loosened from the place it inhabited, it may seem strange, alien. A memento or photograph will now seem oddly different, as if it were not quite what it had been. Beyond the once familiar image, we sense the presence of something else, unrepresentable, opaque, a hole in our psychical world. We acknowledge, at an unconscious level, that part of the one we love *was always lost*, even when they were with us.

In a long and agonizing mourning for the man who had left her, a woman describes a key turning point. She dreams that she is with him and they are looking at an artwork in a cavern. The work is a representation of him. The next moment, they are both inside the artwork, yet still they are looking at a representation of him. As she moves past the image, she sees it turn from a realistic image of him into something more abstract, a streak of colour, something she could only qualify as 'non-representational'. The dream, most obviously, is about her image of him, yet it focuses on precisely a *change* in this image. As well as illustrating the idea we discussed earlier of the frame – the emphasis in the dream on representations as representations (the *mise en abyme* artwork) – it also dramatizes the split between the human image and something opaque and enigmatic beyond it, something ungraspable.

This non-representational element is perhaps the closest we can come to sensing the lost object. Lacan called this the *object a* – a point of emptiness and loss that eludes ready visualization or representation. To apprehend it, Lacan thought, we use our own bodily experiences of loss, as if to find ways to situate it psychically. We unconsciously connect separations linked to feeding and excretion, for example, with the basic dimension of loss established in our early relations with the mother. Since both the breast and excrement are separated from our bodies, they can be used to embody the idea of a loss, to give substance to it. Thus, these elements go into the place of the *object a*, and come to organize the field of our desires. We might cling desperately to our partner, always wanting more and feeling that they have failed to provide us with what we need. Our partner here is like a breast. The anal object, on the other hand, might be at play if we oscillate between love and hate of our partner, rejecting them with disgust at one moment and then adoring them at the next. Our partner here is like shit, both shunned with revulsion and valued as a source of infantile interest.

These hidden objects can never be fully revealed: they are always out of reach, operating none the less to shape our lives and based on a more primary loss. They are veiled behind the visual images that we privilege when we are attracted to others, and which are often moulded by our narcissism. We might fall for someone who looks like we do (think of Brad Pitt and Jennifer Aniston for example) or who looks like the person we want to look like or believe we once did look like. These are all forms of narcissistic love since they involve the projection of our own image on to our partners. We see only ourselves or the way in which we would wish to be seen. Although we might choose a partner following this narcissistic model, the way we actually *relate to them* will be shaped by our relation to the *object a*. There is a tension, then, between narcissism and the object. Narcissism involves the images we identify with and aspire to, while the object is always beyond this, uncanny and ungraspable.

Mourning, Lacan thought, is not about giving up an object but about restoring one's links to an object as lost, as impossible. The key here is to distinguish the object from the narcissistic envelope that covers it, the details of the human image that our love has been drawn to. If the links to the object are restored, and the place of the imaginary envelope separated from this, it may become possible for another to take its place. The problem for the mourner, Lacan argued, is that of maintaining links to the image, through which love is narcissistically structured. If we have loved someone on the model of our own image or drawn them into the field of our own narcissism, then losing them will mean losing ourselves. Hence we refuse to give them up.

This will mean that the object and the place of the object cannot be properly separated out. We will remain tied to the image of the one we love, unable to go beyond this. The image will exert a tyranny over us. We still expect to see them, glimpsing them in the street, hearing their voice in a café, or searching for partners who evoke them. Mourning, in contrast, would imply a certain sacrifice, a sacrifice of our own links to the image. A sacrifice involves the voluntary giving-up of something dear to us. Many burial rites and mourning rituals involve the bereaved's abandonment of a part of him- or herself, be it in the form of a lock of hair or some other object thrown into the grave or tomb. The mourner's hair, unlike the mourner, will stay with the dead. But should we interpret these gestures as an effort to remain inwardly bound to the dead, or, on the contrary, to separate from them?

These small symbolic sacrifices indicate a positive act. As if in addition to what we are forced to lose, we add another loss, as if to positivize it, as if we are *consenting* to the loss rather than refusing it. In the film

Titanic the heroine can finally accept her lover's death many years later when she throws the jewellery so linked to their romance into the sea. And in *Marathon Man*, the gun so strongly bound up with the father is thrown away. It is as if a part of the self is abandoned here, just as the part of oneself in the loved one is abandoned. One loss is added to another, as if to seal a consent.

These ideas all imply that we *are*, in some senses, the one we mourn, and that our love for them was also a love of ourselves. They are part of us. Wouldn't this explain the peculiar phenomenon sometimes found in children who have experienced the loss of a parent: rather than immediate sadness or anger, they feel *ashamed*. If the parent was in fact a part of themselves, as Martha Wolfenstein pointed out, losing them means losing an inalienable possession. We could also see the little sacrifices at the graveside as representative of the much larger sacrifice of consenting to give up a part of ourselves. Mourning must mark out the place of a symbolic sacrifice, so that other objects can go into the place of the lost loved one. This may be the same thing as the big Oedipal sacrifice that structures our childhoods: we renounce the mother in order to gain access to others. Perhaps this must be worked through and re-enacted in any mourning. Real, empirical sacrifices will then function as metaphors of this more fundamental process.

Ang Lee's film of *Brokeback Mountain* illustrates many of these themes. Ostensibly a film about gay cowboys, it is in fact a study of love – and loss – in the widest possible sense. Two young men, Ennis and Jack, are drawn together as they work as cattle-hands one summer on Brokeback Mountain, and their love continues over the next twenty years despite long periods of separation and the obstructions of their respective marriages. At the end of the first summer, after their love has become apparent and physical, they wrestle on a hillside just before they are due to part. As well as affection, the play-fighting evokes fury, not only at the imminent separation but, certainly for Ennis, at the fact that he has fallen in love against his will. The rough and tumble is playful and deadly serious at the same time: each draws blood from the other.

As the story continues, the characters are shown inhabiting a world of discord and compromise. Ennis and Jack are both caught in unhappy marriages and unfulfilling jobs, pining for the moments when they will be able to see each other again. Their trips to the mountains seem blissful: alone with each other at last, away from the trials of their domestic lives, close to the beauty of nature. When Ennis learns of Jack's death, he visits Jack's parents, perhaps with the thought of taking their son's ashes to scatter on Brokeback Mountain in accordance with his wishes. After a strained scene with the parents, Jack's mother invites him to go up to the room he had inhabited as a boy, which she has kept the same ever since.

After looking at the bare and spartan room, his attention is drawn to a recess where he sees the jacket Jack had worn on their first trips. When he looks closer, he sees that behind it is the shirt he, Ennis, had worn on the day they had wrestled. It is hanging inside the shirt that Jack himself wore, and the dried blood-stains are still upon it. Ennis had believed at the time that he'd left the shirt on Brokeback Mountain, but now he realizes that Jack had kept it all along, a secret, stolen token of their love.

Although the film had focused on the clandestine nature of their relationship, conducted behind closed doors in a homophobic society, the scene of the discovery of the shirt demonstrates, on the contrary, that the secret was in fact *inside* the relationship. It was not just the relationship itself that had to be kept hidden, but something within it. The two shirts hanging together embodied the perfect union that could happen not to animate human beings but only to their effigies, the shirts themselves. The fact that the shirt had been purloined and hidden for so long suggests that this was the fantasy that the relationship was predicated on from the start: as if, in some sense, they had both been dead already. The shirts were a supplement that allowed the relationship to endure, the vehicle of a fantasy. We grasp now that all the discord and turmoil surrounding the characters in the outside world was in fact nothing but the externalization of their own internal friction that the fantasy had protected them from.

This startling moment of reversal shows the separation of the object from its envelopes. In the final scene of the film, Ennis's daughter visits him to announce that she is getting married. When she leaves, we see that she has left her sweater behind, and Ennis takes it and secretes it away in a cupboard, just as Jack must have taken his own shirt all those years before. In the face of losing his daughter, he keeps a part of her as a sign of their union, although such a union, of course, has only existed in fantasy. The shirt and the sweater are tokens of something that could never really exist, a harmonious bond of human beings untroubled by strife and sorrow. It is the gap between the shirts and the reality of the relationship that illustrates the idea of the constitution of the object as lost, as impossible. A fundamental emptiness becomes visible in that fleeting, shocking moment of discovery.

——

The idea of a constitution of the object can also be illuminated by the phenomenon of anticipatory grief. Anticipatory grief usually refers to the feelings experienced by those waiting for someone to die. Knowing their loved one is dying, they start the mourning process before the actual death. We sometimes hear it said after a bereavement that the mourning had already taken place: the person had already died for them. This is often heard from the carers of those suffering from Alzheimer's. They were no longer themselves, and this absence was mourned before the moment of biological death itself.

But is this really the essence of anticipatory grief? It could be argued that anticipatory grief is in fact a phenomenon that occurs when the one we are mourning is very far from death. We can find it at those moments when a child realizes that the loved parent will not be there one day. This troubling realization may make a child both sad and furious at the parent. Families are often perplexed at a sudden change in the child's behaviour when they are grappling with this question, especially if the child says nothing about it at the time. Yet they become preoccupied with questions of absence and mortality, which may be glimpsed in little unexplained surges of love towards the parent.

The result of anticipatory grief is the painful realization that the object already contains the possibility of its non-existence. A nothingness is created. And isn't this exactly what we saw in the debate about childhood mourning? Loss can only be mourned, we are told, when we have an idea of a person – but doesn't the very idea of a person contain the idea of that person's absence? The child must confront this awful spectre, which may be elaborated in the later form of a terror of ghosts and the supernatural. Even before the loved one is gone, the ghost of their disappearance is set into place. We can observe this phenomenon in adulthood when someone falls in love. They may suddenly become devastated at the idea that their partner will no longer be there one day, even if at the time they are perfectly present and manifestly devoted. In Apollonius's drama *Argonautica*, Medea loves Jason so much that she says she mourns him as if he were already dead.

This idea of absence is voiced not only in classical drama but also in philosophy. Thousands of books and articles have been devoted to Aristotle's logic, yet the basic, emotional problems he may have been grappling with seem to have gone completely unnoticed. The famous example of a syllogism, 'All men are mortal –

Socrates is a man – Therefore Socrates is mortal', is not simply an abstract logical proposition but a statement about a real, live human being with whom Aristotle had a powerful relationship, even if the two had never met. If today a philosopher wrote a whole book in which the central example concerned the death of his intellectual master, we would surely pick up the emotional subtext. And that this question of mortality is at the heart of Aristotle's concerns becomes even clearer if we remember his much-debated claim 'If a thing may be, it may also not be.' Isn't this, in fact, already a formulation of anticipatory grief?

When later philosophers ponder this question, it seems probable that their own unconscious reactions to loss play a part in the positions they defend sometimes so passionately. Bertrand Russell famously stated that 'The world can be described without the use of the word "not"' and that there are no negative states of affairs or facts. What appeared to be negative could always be rethought as a positive. But this naive view obscures the presence of the negative within the positive: doesn't the positive only really take on its value when we understand that it might not be there for ever? That the person we love could always be absent.

Anticipatory grief can occur quite late in life. Sometimes a person who has had several lengthy relationships will experience it after decades of feeling no similar sentiment. And it can occur quite frequently in relation to parents. An adult will start to distance him- or herself from an ageing parent, sometimes not being fully aware of this. What seems to be a sign of lack of interest or neglect may in fact conceal quite the opposite: they withdraw as if to somehow preserve the parent, to keep them always there, the same for ever. That way they avoid the inevitable failings of the parent's image through age and ill-health.

Freud touches on this idea of an anticipatory grief in his brief paper 'On Transience', written some nine months after the draft of *Mourning and Melancholia* in 1915. When we think about the transience of an object, there is a 'foretaste of mourning over its decease'. Time and mortality are closely bound up here, but also the sensation of love. And could it be that the emergence of anticipatory grief is a part of the birth of human love itself? Does love always involve this 'foretaste of mourning'?

—

The death of a parent or someone truly loved can produce another strange and little-discussed phenomenon. Loss is very often followed by intense sexual desires. The mourner may have images of wild, unrestrained sex and debauchery with a variety of partners, and sexual thoughts are experienced with an unusual intensity and frequency. This can naturally enough generate feelings of guilt and disgust, just as it may result in either guilty inhibition or unrestrained acting out. It ought to be the last thing the person is thinking about. How can we make sense of this disturbing intrusion of sexuality?

The obvious interpretation would be to say that promiscuity and dissipation are simply mechanisms of denial. We search frantically for substitutes for the lost loved one, to obliterate our feelings of loss, and to cover over the hole of an absence with physical, carnal proximity. While there is no doubt sometimes a manic side to such behaviour, and a clear sense of a denial of loss, it still leaves open the question of why such behaviour sometimes occurs much later on in the mourning process. If we explore these cases carefully, we find that what appears to be dissipation is actually quite the opposite. If many partners might be sought early on after a loss, what happens later is very different: it tends to focus not on the many but the one.

In some cultures which still adhere to formal mourning rituals, the period of mourning is completed by a sexual act. The mourner is actually obliged to have sexual relations, whether they like it or not. This has been interpreted as a kind of purification via sex. Bits of semen or vaginal secretion remain lodged in the body of the deceased's spouse, and these must be removed to render them harmless. The sexual traces of the dead person have to be cast off. The mourner must be purified of them in order to become distanced from the malevolent influence of the dead. Sex with another partner allows this, and the partner in question will then have to go through a further purification ritual to create even more distance from the dead. In some cultures, the body is covered in thick paste or dyes to help remove every sexual trace of the deceased.

If such practices might seem peculiar, we should remember how Western medieval romance is packed with bereaved heroines who refuse to cut their hair or to wash, hugging their dirt and bodily residues as a way of remaining close to the lost loved one. This has often been interpreted as an identification with the dead, as if the mourner makes herself an outcast just as the body of her lover has been literally removed from human society. And it would imply logically that in order to give up the loved one, the dirt has to be given up first.

In Kieslowski's film *Blue*, Juliette Binoche plays a young woman whose husband and child are killed in a car crash. As she struggles to continue her life and separate herself from the world of the dead, she spends the night with a man trying to complete her late husband's unfinished work. She doesn't want a relationship, yet somehow this sexual act frees her. She is now able to work on the symphony her husband had been composing. There is an echo here of the rites we have mentioned in which mourners have to rid themselves of something linked to the dead: whether it is vaginal secretions or sperm, it must be passed on and hence made distant.

But does this really explain the sexual act here? It could equally be linked with the idea of a triumph in mourning. At some level we have got what we wanted, and so there is a sudden release of triumph and joy. We had a death-wish and now it is satisfied. But we may also be exuberant simply to have avoided the same fate ourselves, to have survived. Freud noted how funerary rituals nearly always included a special meal, in which the dead were symbolically consumed, indicating not only an incorporation but also a celebratory victory. Looking at it from another angle, could the libido released in such instances be the same libido that had been bound up with the lost loved one and which is now set free?

Perhaps it would be a mistake, however, to see Binoche's sexual act as altogether sexual. If it was not just about bodily pleasure, it may have a link to the idea of a sacrifice. What does she do, after all, if not *give herself*? And doesn't this mean that she no longer belongs to her dead husband? To free herself from him, she has first to free herself from herself. Which means discarding her own image, her own body, by lending it to another man. Mourning here involves a moulting of oneself.

—

The fourth element of the mourning process concerns who it is we are mourning for. We might take it for granted that when we mourn, we are mourning the one we've lost. We think of them, we see their image, we hear their voice, and they are present to us in so many painful and poignant ways. While this is certainly the case, we may also be mourning something else. Lacan made a very interesting observation here. He pointed out that mourning is not just about mourning the lost loved one, but about mourning *who we were for them*.

A woman mourning the death of her mother spoke of a feeling that kept returning to her, despite her unease at its apparent triviality. Although she was immersed in images and thoughts of her mother and her illness, these would repeatedly converge on one simple moment: when her mother would use a nickname for her, 'Sparrow'. 'I realized,' she said, 'that no one would ever call me that again.' This special designation was only used by her mother, and it was this that kept returning, rather than, as one might have expected, her own nickname for the mother. What haunted her was not just the image of her mother but the privileged point at which her own image was composed for the Other.

We spend our lives, after all, actively caught up in relationships. When we love other people, we have a place in the relationships we forge with them. Just as we give them a place, so the very fabric of our relationship to them accords us a place. It gives us a certain identity, as a child to be loved, to be mistreated, to be listened to, ignored or whatever image has been given a special value in our unconscious mental life. We create relationships in part in order to secure imaginary positions for ourselves. The function of a relationship is, in part, to maintain this position: it situates us as an image in relation to the gaze of someone else.

After several years of agonizing grief following the separation from her beloved partner, a woman began a new relationship. She had never imagined meeting a man she could care for again, and her feelings of attraction to the new boyfriend both troubled and confused her. She realized that she was in completely new territory, since she did not know, as she put it, 'who I am' outside the relationship with her previous love. Even after their separation, she had continued life as if they were together, defining herself in relation to him and seeing herself through his eyes. Finding words to describe the new relationship was almost impossible for her: 'It's like an empty space,' she said. It was soon after this encounter with the new man that she decided to visit a far-flung region of the world, known for its barren geography, as if she had to literally inhabit an empty space before she could start to make sense of what she was feeling.

Relationships give us places and when they end we have to decide whether we can give up these places or not. When we do manage to loosen the bonds to the one we have lost, this will mean loosening the bonds to the image we took up in that relationship. And this can even affect our actual body image. The painter L. S. Lowry was caught up in a powerful relation of dependence with his demanding mother, and throughout his life he would say that everything he did had a meaning only for her. During her fatal illness, he found himself looking into his shaving mirror, seeing a strange face staring back at him. This alienation from his own image was experienced by Lowry as he painted a series of staring male heads during the same period. He would say that these heads 'just happened'. Rather than being crafted with design, they just appeared on the canvas, and many years later he could still ask a visitor to his studio, 'What do they mean?'

What connected Lowry to his body image, what made the image his own, was linked to his relation with his mother. As her sanctioning or condemning look threatened to disappear, so his own links to his body image evaporated. The place that his image occupied for her had changed, and so it lost its anchoring point. This renunciation of the image is rarely as literal as it was for Lowry, but the questioning of one's identity can take other forms. A mourner may forget their own phone number, their address or to carry their identity papers. As Joan Didion noticed, 'For forty years I saw myself through John's eyes.' But now that he was gone, this perspective was put in question: 'This year for the first time since I was twenty-nine I saw myself through the eyes of others.' As she writes, 'when we mourn our losses we also mourn, for better or for worse, ourselves. As we were. As we are no longer. As we will one day not be at all.'

Yet this is hardly ever clear for us. We have to give up what we were for the one we've lost, but much of this will have been structured at an unconscious level. As one mourner put it, 'In order to be able to give up a relation, I need to know what that relation is.' And this is yet another reason why the work of mourning is so long and painful. It involves, after all, a real giving up of a part of ourselves. We are forced to relinquish our own image. Describing the grief and mourning following the death of his son, Gordon Livingstone observes how his own self-image as an admired father had been lost: 'Just beneath the anger is my bottomless sadness that the one person who loved me without reservation is gone. I tell myself that he could not indefinitely have believed I was perfect, but I miss that so.'

Perhaps this is the reason why some people will actually change their appearance during the process of mourning. They may adopt a new haircut or style of dress. And also why it is quite common that when people speak about the moment of learning of a loss they may have no recollection at all of the words used or the precise information conveyed, yet remember exactly what they were wearing, some trivial detail of their clothes. Although we could obviously explain this in terms of a displacement, a kind of denial of the reality of the bad news and a shift to the contingent detail of the garment, doesn't it also suggest a refocus towards one's own image? As if the news of the loss involved, at some level, a questioning of this image?

This feature of mourning can help to explain a peculiar custom associated most often with Jewish tradition but found also in other cultures. After a death, the mirrors in the house of the grieving family are covered up. The common-sense interpretation of this practice is to see the removal of mirror images as a reminder that we must give up our vanity at times of grief. At a deeper level, it has been claimed that the shrouding serves to keep the dead at bay: if they hover menacingly in the house they once inhabited, they may be confused by their own image and so decide to take up residence once again. But don't we also see here a connection between the loss of a loved one and the loss of our own image? Giving them up means giving up the image of who we were for them: and this will have a profound effect on our self-image.

When we lose a loved one, we have lost a part of ourselves. And this loss requires our *consent*. We might well tell ourselves that we have accepted a loss, but acquiescence and true consent are fundamentally different. Many people, indeed, go through life obeying others while harbouring a burning resentment within themselves. They say `Yes' without meaning it, in the same way that a small child might follow the demands of potty training out of fear, without ever having really agreed to them. In mourning, we have to consent at the deepest level to the loss of a part of ourselves, and that's why, as we have seen, it involves an additional sacrifice. It implies logically that the only way to give up the image we took on for someone else is to question the way we imagined they looked at us. The film *Blue* provides another example here. The character played by Juliette Binoche finds out after the accident in which her husband and child die that he had in fact been leading a double life. He had been having an affair and his mistress was now about to have his child. She thus not only has to mourn him, but the image she had *for him*, of what she was for him, even if she only really discovers this after the death.

We find a similar reversal in the mourning of Queen Victoria for her mother, who died less than a year before her beloved husband Albert. Victoria's mourning for Albert preoccupied both the public and her later biographers, as it seemed quite spectacular in its refusal to accept his absence. But this has obscured the crucial question of how she responded to her mother's death. Victoria had always believed herself to be unimportant for her mother: in her journal, she would write 'I don't believe Ma. ever loved me.' But after her death, as she went through her mother's papers, she discovered that even the tiniest mementoes and scraps of writing she had authored had been kept. She was overwhelmed to realize that she had indeed been the object of maternal love, and now felt an acute regret over the lost opportunities for reciprocating.

The image she had of herself was thus profoundly transformed. Where the character played by Binoche had to give up who she imagined herself to be as a wife, Victoria confronted a change in her self-image as a daughter. The breakdown that followed, together with her prolonged, excessive grief for her husband, suggest that perhaps her mourning for Albert contained within it the unseen effort to mourn her own mother. And didn't this protracted process put her in the very place she had not been able to occupy for her mother while alive? That of the devoted, loving daughter. She would refer to Albert, after all, as having been 'a mother' to her, and after his death compare herself to 'a child that has lost its mother'.

Returning to the problem of the sexual encounter in *Blue*, couldn't we now interpret it in a different way? On one level, there is an identification with the dead. Just as the husband had been unfaithful, now so is the wife, as if to say 'You weren't who I thought you were, so now, neither am I!' But at another, perhaps deeper level, we could interpret her making love with the man as an act of giving herself, in the specific sense of giving up her image. After this sacrifice, she attains a new freedom.

⸺

Having an idea of who we are for others is hardly simple. Sophie Calle illuminates this question in her own unique way. Her work is perpetually concerned with her own image. She will hire private detectives to follow her, describing and recording her movements. She is interested in how she is constituted for others, how they see her. In some works, she becomes a character in someone else's fiction, allowing others to choose her itineraries for her. She once asked the writer Paul Auster to dictate what she'd do for a year, and when he replied by prescribing a more modest series of tasks, she undertook all of them. She even followed a diet he set for her, whereby each day she would have to eat only food of a certain colour.

This project could be seen as a kind of parody of Modernism. Just as in the Modernist novel, protagonists and narrators are so often cold and detached from the events they describe, here Calle turns herself into a character from whom she is always creating distance. Her very identity is mapped through other people, and the things that happen *in* her life are depicted as things that happen *to* her. In fact, despite orchestrating plenty of scenarios, she never presents herself as an author of her actions, but rather as the product of other people's actions and choices.

Beyond this interesting inflection of Modernism, Calle's work poses the question of how she emerges through the narrative of others. Who, she seems to be asking, is her author? This exploration of who she is for others can be linked to a moment in her childhood that she sees as a turning point. Finding a letter from a family friend to her mother referring to 'our Sophie', she wondered what this could mean. What was the sense of the possessive pronoun here? In what way could she be 'our'? She wondered, indeed, if this man was in fact her true father, and a web of fantasy and daydream was spun from this point between the ages of eight and eleven. This pronoun set the direction of her artistic practice: a questioning of who she is for the other, how she can be seen, perceived, filmed, looked at, and thought about by someone else.

In her art, Calle also stages artificial attachments to strangers. Choosing someone at random, she would follow them and document their behaviour in the utmost detail. Then she would leave the scene, never, in principle, to see them again. This concentration of her emotions would make them, she says, both 'arbitrary and real'. She would be profoundly attached to that person, 'if only for half an hour'. After that time, the spell would be broken. If the encounter had ended in a necessary separation, this was a separation that 'doesn't hurt'.

It is difficult not to think here of the cotton-reel game described by Freud that fascinated so many later generations of analysts. Watching his grandson pull a cotton-reel towards him and then throw it away, Freud believed he was witnessing an archaic process of symbolizing the mother's presence and absence. The reel stood for the mother, and by making it appear and disappear, the boy was making himself the master of a situation over which he could otherwise have little control.

The key to this game, however, did not lie simply in the repeated activity but in the fact that the cotton-reel's movements were accompanied by sounds: the boy would utter the word 'da' (there) when the reel was present and 'fort' (gone) when it was not. He wasn't just creating a rhythm of presence and absence, but was actively linking this to a symbolic process, to words and the difference between the two terms he had chosen. The mother's absence was thus being taken up into a symbolic network. It was being registered in language.

Calle's artificial attachments are like the game with the cotton-reel. As well as generating presence and absence, they involve registration, since her work consists in making records of her activities. She doesn't just follow people, she documents and marks the attachments with notes and photos. 'My movements', she says, 'were dictated by decisions to do with leaving men and being with men.' If these moments of separation and loss were so important for her, her work provides a kind of mimicry of the mourning process. Absence is registered and recorded, even if the question of her own identity, of who she is for others, is never finally answered.

—

This aspect of the mourning process also gives us a clue to a clinical problem that intrigued Freud. Why, he wondered, did mourning involve not just depressed states but also anxious ones? Tennyson had posed a similar question many years previously in his poem 'In Memoriam' when he had asked 'Can calm despair and wild unrest / be tenants of a single breast?' It is a fact that where one person may respond to a loss with a general inertia and lack of vitality, another may feel a sense of persistent anxiety, as if something terrible is just about to happen, a sort of expectant dread. In many cases, the depressed and anxious states are mixed together. How can we understand these clinical phenomena?

Anxiety, according to Lacan, is the sensation of the desire of the Other. It means that we are confronted with the question of what we are for them, what value we have for the Other, the first model of which is the primary caregiver of our infancy. This can be played out again with any figure in our later life, from our lovers and spouses to our bosses and workmates. If we find ourselves in some situation where we are suddenly no longer sure of our bearings, with no idea of where we stand or how we are being perceived, the response may well be a feeling of anxiety. Now, what does this have to do with mourning?

It often happens that a person will find a way of solving a difficult, intolerable situation within a family or in relation to a caregiver by appealing to the image of someone else. This could be a brother or a sister, or someone else in the family who is close at hand. They are followed around, often quite literally, and they may well have been the favourite of the parent in question. We could think here of the case we discussed in Chapter 1 of the woman whose anguish began when the brother whom her mother had so idealized died. Family relations are built around the image of the sibling so that they constitute a barrier between the child and the caregiver.

When this imaginary buffer is withdrawn, through death, separation or illness, suddenly the person is without any defensive barrier. There is no longer any mediation between them and the terrible question of what they are for the Other. And this can trigger an unbearable sense of anguish and dread. The anxiety here is less about the loss of the person in question than about the consequences of this loss in terms of another relationship, usually that with one of the parents. This is the relationship that matters, and that the privileged place given to the sibling *was itself a response to*. With their loss, the mourner is thrown back on to the question of their own identity for someone else. And so – clinically – the rhythm of depression and anxiety that we find so often in mourning.

The example of the image of the sibling is useful here as it brings the triangular situation into focus, but it is just as frequently a question of an image the subject has adopted himself in the relationship with the parent. When this image is called into question – for example, because of the death of a parent – there is no longer any protection or barrier and so anxiety can become overwhelming. The parent dying here does not mean their absence from the psychical world of the mourner: on the contrary, it is well known that death can only make the image of the lost person stronger, and their imperatives more powerful.

⸺

The four elements of mourning we have discussed can be illustrated with a clinical example. A patient had lost his wife a year previously, and had been in a state of inertia since her death, unable to work or carry out his daily activities, haunted by images and memories of her, searching the streets for her image, and unable to maintain links with his friends and family. The sequence we will examine here took place over a six-month period, at the end of which he was able to overcome the severity of his inertial state, resume his work and think anew about the possibilities of living. We can follow his progress through a series of dreams which show how the mourning process was unfolding.

Dream 1: X is furious with his wife, and they have a huge fight. He reproaches her for having failed to disclose a certain piece of information to him. Another woman then enters the scene who has exaggerated traits of his wife. He leaves with her, and as they move through a party, he finds himself behaving with her in the way his wife would behave in public with him. On waking, X contemplates for a moment the visual image of the second woman and realizes suddenly that this is in fact the image of his wife.

Dream 2: X is in the house where he had lived with his wife. He wants a cup of tea but there is no milk. He asks various characters who seem to be hanging around, and is told that there is not enough milk left. He then goes into each room of the house, expecting to find someone there but there is no one. Finally, in the last room, X sees a multitude of belongings set out either in preparation for a trip or indicating the return from a trip. He expects to see his wife, but there's no one there.

Dream 3: X is in a shop. He drops some milk and hopes that the cashier will give him another carton free. She doesn't. He then brings out all his change, but she still refuses. His wife appears and they cling to each other in a very physical, erotic way.

Dream 4: X is with his wife. She says, 'It's a one-way traffic.' X tries to understand what this means. Is it a one-way traffic for him or for his wife? He tries to understand but is unable to. Throughout the dream, X has the profound sensation of not knowing his wife. He then finds himself in a room filled with suitcases. He says either, 'Been somewhere?' or 'Going somewhere?' but cannot remember which.

Dream 5: X is with his wife and again has the sensation of her strangeness. She seems alien, completely opaque. Then she takes hold of him and says, 'Don't ever leave me.' He says, 'I won't,' but isn't actually too sure.

Dream 6: X feels out of place. Then there is simply an image of a piece of white fabric with a small excremental stain on it.

One could certainly approach these dreams from the usual perspectives of popular psychology: the denial of death, the rage, the journey, the parting, etc. But they reveal far more about the unconscious processes that allow mourning to take place. The associations to the dreams were invaluable here, and they brought out important links between his wife, his mother and his own image. The reproach to the wife in the first dream echoed the man's reproach to his mother at a particular moment in his childhood, a reproach of which he had not been conscious until he was associating to the dream. She had departed to go on a long trip, leaving him without warning with his grandparents. His rage and confusion had never been consciously voiced before, and it was only now that he could begin to think about the effects of this early betrayal. It was the loss of his wife that sent him back to this crucial discontinuity in his childhood.

The first dream also elaborates this relation between wife and mother in another way. There is an emphasis on images, as if they could be detached from those who inhabit them: a woman looks like his wife, he behaves as if he were her and then realizes that the other woman is in fact his wife. These are motifs of narcissism, which involves our identifications with images and our capture within them. They are images of who we are or want to be, but the dream shows that these images are just images: the way that they are swapped around signals that they can be somehow loosened from their anchoring point. Images and what lies beyond them, however, are different things. The dream suggests a first step in this basic untangling of the image from what the image comes to envelop.

Dream 2 continues to evoke X's relation to his mother, who had 'run out of milk' after a brief period of breastfeeding him. There is thus a tension between the material linked to narcissism, in which images can be swapped and we can take the place of other people, and that linked to the object – in this case, the oral object – which cannot be swapped or traded. It embodies, on the contrary, a fixity linked to bodily satisfaction. The third dream continues this refinement of the separation of the field of narcissism and the object: when X is confronted with a woman who refuses to give him anything, the image of his wife appears and a bodily enjoyment emerges at the point of frustration. The analytic work during this time was particularly concerned with exploring the links of the image of his wife with that of his mother.

Dreams 4 and 5 are in a way paradigmatic of the mourning process, in demonstrating the separation of the image and another register beyond it. Both of them confront X with the intense sensation of something unknowable about his wife. The question about the meaning of the one-way traffic evoked for X both the one-way journey of his wife and the fact that he too would be taking a one-way journey at some point in the future. His incomprehension can be taken as a sign of the real, where death presents itself as an opaque riddle to which the dreamer – and indeed language itself – has no answer. The questions about the meaning of the baggage also reminded X of the time in his childhood when his mother had left on her trip. These themes are played out again in the fifth dream around the phrase 'Don't ever leave me', which X would say was really his own plea, addressed both to his mother and to his wife.

Before commenting on the apparently incongruous sixth dream, we should say something about X's experience since roughly the time of Dream 4. These months had been characterized by an overcoming of inertia and an almost manic enjoyment of certain jokes, wordplay and anecdotes which he would return to frequently. After Dream 6, X realized that all these actually shared a common theme: a scatological reference to the image of a shitty baby. The shift in the dream from X feeling he doesn't have a place to his total eclipse in the image of the excrementally marked fabric suggests the equivalence of X to excrement: this is the image of what is out of place, what shouldn't be there. At that moment, X remembered a detail from the period during which he had first met his wife. Before the dinner at which he had been introduced to her, he had heard a story about a holiday scene in which she had apparently relieved herself in an un-inhibited display in front of other people. In the following weeks, X would remember his own efforts to hide his excretory activities as a child from everyone but his mother.

I did not interpret X's dreams, not just because they were interpreted by X himself, but because, like many of the dreams we find punctuating the mourning process, they were interpretations in themselves. Although we might choose to find in them the anal dynamics that so interested Abraham, it seems to me that they stage the split between the field of narcissistic identification and the object emphasized by Lacan. In the dream series, we see a separation of the image of the wife from the oral and anal registers, and, in the associations, the thread that made this woman take the place in his phantasy that she held for so long, a thread that was partly bound to the field of narcissism as we can see in the detail of the wife's scatalogical exhibitionism that appealed so much to him. This was the image he himself aspired to, showing his excrement proudly to his mother.

This separation meant the emergence of a deep sense of alterity. As the image lost its usual co-ordinates, he could feel the otherness, the enigma of his wife, and no doubt this evoked for him too the alterity of his mother. In the sixth dream, we see how the lack of a representation responds to the point of real loss. And, at the end of the sequence, in X's new interest in life, we see, broadly speaking, the reintegration of the object in its narcissistic framework. They had been separated during the work of mourning, but now they could start to function together once more: he could become attracted to the images of other women, and he felt that they held something enticing.

These dreams also illustrate the dialectic of desires that Lacan put at the heart of the mourning process. The opacity of the woman and her enigmatic pronouncement index the dimension of the desire of the Other, that part of the mother's subjectivity that was never satisfied with her child. The question here concerns, as Lacan put it, to what extent the subject was a lack for the Other, that is, what place they had in the Other's desire. Although X's 'Don't ever leave me' is ascribed to the wife, her ineffable and opaque presence in the previous dreams was experienced as a fundamental non-recognition, indicating that her desire was aimed ultimately beyond him.

When Lacan observed that we can only mourn someone of whom we can say 'I was their lack', it implies precisely this question of what we were for the Other. Being someone's lack means that they have projected their own sense of lack on to you: in other words, they love you. We love, after all, those who seem to have something we don't. In this sense, part of the work of mourning involves mourning the imaginary object that we were for the Other. And isn't hatred one of the consequences of not being able to say 'I was their lack': exactly what blocks the mourning process according to Freud? The dream sequence also illuminates another important moment. There was certainly a sense of frustration for X and, at the end of the sequence, a new interest in life, but in between there was a very deep experience of his wife's alterity, her otherness. How, we could ask, can we ever detach ourselves from those we have lost without recognizing this ungraspable, enigmatic dimension?

Curiously, this part of the work of mourning is a central thread in a certain tradition of Catholicism. So many authors, from Augustine onwards, emphasize how, in order to recognize the strangeness of God, we must first confront our strangeness to ourselves. This realization will involve not only contemplation but also violence and pain, as we are torn away from our beloved self-image and its reflections. As Saint John of the Cross put it, it is only when God has become wholly and terrifyingly a stranger to us that we can ever really 'know' Him as something beyond a projection of our own wants. This is exactly the tension between the unknowable, opaque dimension of our loved ones and the narcissistic coating that we have given them. It is when we can see them as more than the echo of ourselves that they emerge as truly real for the first time.

—

Let's take another example here to clarify the significance in mourning of the sense of alterity and of a register beyond visual images. Rather than a clinical case, it is a historical account discussed by Richard Trexler in his book on everyday life in medieval Florence and also by Jean-Claude Schmitt in his study of ghosts in the Middle Ages. Giovanni Morelli was a Florentine born in 1372, whose eldest son Alberto died at the age of nine in 1406. No priest had been present at the deathbed and Giovanni became more and more convinced that he had deserted his son. He avoids

Alberto's room for the next six months, and, despite conscious efforts not to think about him, the image of the son was ever present: 'We continually have his image before our eyes, remember his ways, his conditions, words and acts, day and night, at lunch and dinner, inside and out.' It is as if the dead boy is tormenting them: 'We think he is holding a knife that is stabbing us in the heart.'

On the first anniversary of Alberto's death, this pain became unbearable: 'It seemed to me my soul with my body was tormented by a thousand lance tips.' Giovanni chastises himself for not having had the boy's confession heard, although we know that in contemporary Florence Alberto had not yet reached the age for first confession. Giovanni thought that it was because of his neglect that the image of Alberto was haunting him. At the exact time of his son's death, he gazed fixedly at the images of Christ, Mary and the Evangelist, embracing and kissing them in the same places that his son had. Staring at these images, he reviewed in his mind the sorrow that they would have undergone, and then the catalogue of his own faults, before praying to them for Alberto's salvation.

After this ritual, Giovanni couldn't sleep. Lying there, tossing and turning in bed, he imagined that the Devil was trying to convince him that his efforts had been in vain and was urging him to think about his own life and unhappiness. Giovanni then gave up the decision to think only of Alberto, and allowed Satan to set out before him the story of his own life. At the moment he agrees to think about himself and not just about Alberto, the turmoil passes. Satan lists all the losses that Giovanni has experienced: his father, his mother, his sister, his first love, his money, his property, and so on. The Devil here is doing exactly what Melanie Klein had claimed was central to the mourning process: running through all of the earlier losses that preceded the most recent one.

Satan tells him that the best thing that ever happened to him was the birth of his son, which has now become his greatest sorrow. Giovanni then reproaches himself: 'You didn't treat him as a son but as an outsider . . . You never once showed him a happy face. You never once kissed him so that he thought it affectionate.' This self-reproach is typical of Giovanni, and we know that a great deal of his time was spent in lamenting the history of sorrow and dejection in his family. Just as his own father had been mistreated by his family, so, he thought, life had dealt him a cruel hand.

Giovanni himself had been abandoned by his father, who had died when he was two. His mother had remarried soon afterwards, leaving her children with her parents. When he had set about writing the biography of his father, Giovanni had assumed that the latter had been as little loved by his own father as Giovanni supposes he was by his. He stresses again and again his father's deprivation, unhappiness and victimization. When Giovanni turns to his own life, the same sense of failure runs through it. Abandoned time and time again, the damages he had suffered from the injuries of his childhood were 'neither imaginable, nor recordable, but infinite'.

Returning to the nocturnal sequence, Giovanni feels

suicidal, and now compares his suffering to that of Christ. This idea of not being entirely alone allows him to drift into sleep. Then a dream vision proves to him that his earlier prayer had been heard: he is told that the death had not been his fault. In the first part of the vision, he is plagued by the image of Alberto. To get rid of it, he decides to walk around a local high point, Monte Morello, linked linguistically to his own family name. On the walk, he can think only of Alberto and especially of his own failure in relation to his son. As he becomes more and more tormented, he loses track of time. After a while, the torment is replaced by sweet memories of Alberto's birth and infancy. A host of positive images emerge.

Giovanni sits down to weep when a bird flies down from the mountain, singing sweet melodies. But as Giovanni approaches it, the melodies become hideous and he flees. As he does so, the bird is attacked by a sow, covered in muck from a boar, which he describes as a horrible experience. Then he sees two starlike lights in the distance, and, moving towards them, he kneels down and prays for an explanation. A brilliant light surrounds him, which turns out to be his special saint, Catherine. A cloud of birds approaches, and one of them is transformed into Alberto. Giovanni turns towards this apparition and, realizing that it can't be physically grasped, starts speaking to it. The spirit of Alberto tells him that his prayers have been accepted, and in response to Giovanni's question 'Am I the cause of your death?' tells him that it wasn't his fault. It says to him 'Do not seek the impossible.'

This beautiful sequence illustrates many of the

themes we have discussed: the recording of an absence, the running through of earlier losses, the putting of oneself in the position of the dead, and the appeal to a third party to authenticate and mediate a loss. Curiously, the account given by Richard Trexler leaves out some even more suggestive details. The bird had in fact fallen from its branch, and the sow, which the boar has just befouled, passes over it and covers it in excrement. The encounter which follows with the dazzling white beauty of the saint is marked by the fact that she cuts the sow into pieces. The references to excrement and violence seem out of place, yet they form an essential part of Giovanni's dream experience.

Here are all the motifs dear to Klein and Abraham: the emergence of the register of anality, the attacks on the mother's body, and so forth. But can't we also see mapped out the split between the narcissistic, beautiful shining image and the object, here in the form of the fallen, excremental residue? At this decisive moment in the mourning process, Giovanni's dream enacts a series of separations, as if to represent the difference between the cherished image – that of his lost son – and another register that lies beyond this. Crucial here is the description of the transformation of the bird into Alberto: at the same time as constituting his son, there is something ungraspable about this image. As in the clinical sequence we discussed earlier, we witness a separation of two registers in Giovanni's mourning: the image is prised apart from an alterity that lies beyond it. And this process has a tempering, mediating effect on the mourner's suffering.

4

We have explored four processes which signal that the work of mourning is taking place: the introduction of a frame to mark out a symbolic, artificial space, the necessity of killing the dead, the constitution of the object – involving the separation of the image of the loved one and the place they occupied for us – and the giving up of the image of who we were for them. These four motifs show some of the differences between grief – our emotional reaction to a loss – and mourning, which is a kind of psychical work. But what would happen if these processes were unavailable or blocked? When we look in detail at individual cases of mourning, we see that in fact they are nearly always somehow impeded. They may certainly develop with time, but these unconscious processes are never as smooth as many accounts of the neat stages of mourning suggest.

Freud believed that the main barrier to the work of mourning was the mixture of hatred with love. The more that our positive feelings towards the one we'd lost are swamped with negative ones, the more difficult it is to separate ourselves from them. Hatred, indeed, is a strong human bond, and we all know from our daily lives how anger and fury at another person are hardly compatible with forgetting them. But for Freud, a blocked, interrupted or failed mourning is not the same thing as melancholia. If both involve problems in dealing with loss, melancholia is still a rather different clinical category.

As we saw in Chapter 1, melancholia is distinguished by the severe changes in a person's self-regard. The melancholic will see him- or herself as worthless and irrevocably guilty. Nothing can change the fixity of this self-image, which may attain a delusional certainty. Freud explained this with the idea of an all-encompassing identification with the lost person: the reproaches to the other become reproaches to oneself. This was taken to be the central defining trait of melancholia, yet it was also what his students Abraham and Klein both disagreed with him about. They did not see self-reproach as resulting exclusively from having identified with the loved and hated lost object. Self-reproach, they thought, was much more than simply a turning of a reproach directed outside back towards the self. Before going any further, let's take a clinical example.

A woman in her mid-forties described the self-reproaches that had progressively invaded her life. Her initial complaint had been intense anxiety states, which she did not understand, and fears about the inside of her body. These fears in fact formed part of her battery of self-reproaches, which she was able to divide up into more or less three different groups. The first set of reproaches involved the conviction that she had done something wrong, although she didn't know what. The second set consisted of the reproach that she was 'horrible', 'disgusting'. And the third, and for her the most terrible, that her fate 'was to be alone for ever'.

These reproaches would take the form of conscious thoughts as well as invasive ideas and images that 'pushed their way', as she said, into her mind. The third group of reproaches was the most unbearable for her, and she described the idea of having to 'go on and on for ever after dying' as the most horrific destiny anyone could imagine.

After a long period of analytic work, it became possible to reconstruct the context in which the self-reproaches had emerged. She had suffered a miscarriage twenty years previously, which had been heralded by a bleed. She had been in the house at that time with her mother, and after she had commented on the bleed, her mother had made an equivocal remark about having the baby christened. The miscarriage was followed by a period of silence: her husband and family made no reference to it, and carried on as if nothing had happened. It was from this moment that her sense of life changed: 'I felt like a ghost,' she said, going through the routines of her everyday life numb and devitalized, 'as if I was not alive.'

Several months later, and shortly before what would have been the child's birthdate, as she was walking home from work, she heard a voice which told her she would be dead by the date in question. The voice didn't generate any anxiety in her, but seemed 'natural', as if it formed a part of her everyday reality. She simply accepted its prediction. Soon, however, a second pregnancy took the voice away, and the self-reproaches abated as she raised this child and her subsequent children.

Many years later, a series of unpredictable events

brought back the voice announcing her death, and the self-reproaches took on a more powerful consistency. As she described the different forms of these reproaches and their contexts, it became clear that the first set – which declared her guilt – were a direct derivative of her mother's accusations. Throughout her childhood, she had always been the one at fault in the mother's eyes. Whatever she did, the mother criticized her for not doing it properly. Later, these accusations would be internalized and turned against herself.

The second set of reproaches also had a clear origin. As she described the horrible, intrusive images of a disgusting body, she realized that this had been a vague thought at the back of her mind at the time of the miscarriage. She had wondered what became of the baby's body, and had conjured up a series of images of the miscarried foetus. The words used to describe these images were exactly those used to describe her own image of herself afterwards, as if the dead child's image had become superimposed on her own body.

The third set of self-reproaches echoed this process. One day, speaking about the ideas of being condemned to eternity, she said suddenly, 'There's no place for you in this world.' The sentence surprised her, and she did not know where it had sprung from. What did 'this world' mean here, she wondered? But then she remembered her fascination and terror as a child on hearing about purgatory in religious education at school. Visions of an endless hell had frightened her, and now the sequence became clearer. The mother's enigmatic reference to the christening had suggested to her that, without a name, a child could not go to heaven but would remain in limbo for eternity. And this was exactly the form of her terror at being alone for ever.

We see here the identification with the lost object described by Freud. After the loss of the baby, its shadow fell on her own ego: she became the dead child, and so the thoughts of the mutilated body and of being condemned to limbo for eternity began to take over her own self-image. Her actual experience of time was thus profoundly affected by the identification, and it drew on what she had learnt as a child about purgatory. The feelings of being a ghost after the miscarriage reflected this precisely: in effect, she had died with her baby.

—

We saw earlier how the work of mourning involves killing the dead. The mourner has the choice of killing the dead or dying with them. The melancholic choice here is to die with the dead. This can be quite literally, as with those suicides that swiftly follow the death of a loved one, or it can occur even while the person remains biologically alive, as we saw with our clinical example. Analysts and psychiatrists are familiar with those cases where someone seems intent on committing suicide, planning the act calmly and methodically. In some cases, this calmness is possible because the person is in fact already dead: the lack of any surface disturbance can mislead the clinician into thinking there is no suicide risk.

The force of Freud's argument here is to show that we can die before our biological death, as we turn to inhabit the world of the dead or departed. The lost loved one is then never relinquished. When clinicians receive patients who seem desolate and dejected, it is always crucial to explore in the greatest detail the history and context of the surface depression. In some cases, what can be easily labelled 'depression' may conceal the fact that the subject has already died with their lost loved one. This may be a response not only to a real bereavement, but to the loss of a lover, a friend or even a political or religious ideal. Several of the medieval medical texts on melancholia, in fact, mention loss of one's books or library as a precipitating factor. What matters is the idea of losing what is most precious. When a clinician receives a supposedly depressed patient, they must explore with a fine-toothed comb to see whether the flatness or sense of mortification conceals a form of death that may subsequently be made real by a suicidal act.

The idea of dying with the dead can explain many other clinical phenomena. The melancholic may complain of illnesses or bodily symptoms which turn out to mirror those of the lost person. Or they may find themselves acting out parts of the life of the lost person, or even experiencing parts of their body as if they belonged to the other. In one case, a man would wake up in the night and see his arms as if they were the arms of someone else. As he searched for words to describe them, the only terms that emerged were those used to describe the arms of the father who had died when he was a child. 'When I awoke my arms were visible to me in reality but they were not mine – they were somehow dead, lacking life, blurred and yellow.

My own real body was the ghost and I was frightened.'
The lost object had literally come to inhabit his body.

Dying with the dead has another consequence here: it means that the dead cannot be killed. And this, as we have seen, will always block the mourning process. It puts the melancholic subject in a very particular position. He is situated in between two worlds: the world of the dead and the world of the living. In the case of the woman discussed above, she felt dead after the miscarriage, as if she were now a ghost. And melancholics so often describe this split existence: on the one hand, a life lived with others in society and groups, and on the other, an absolute solitude. As one man put it: 'It's like sleep-walking, being in two parallel synchronous states of being.' Experiencing this split, trying to make sense of it and articulating it may be a dreadful, unbearably painful process for the melancholic.

This can shed light on the well-known problem of the morning agonies of the melancholic. Why is waking so difficult? Is it because of the prospect of facing another day or is it due to a disturbed brain chemistry? As one melancholic put it, waking was the most painful part of the day because 'it means passing from one world to another'. The border between the world of sleep and that of waking may be experienced as that between the worlds of the dead and the living: and so it brings home all the more acutely the impossibility of their situation.

Sometimes, this split existence involves the feeling that the living are not really alive. Other people are described as empty husks, mere simulacra, unreal shadows. In daily life, the melancholic is forced to carry out everyday routines, make small-talk, pursue a dull job and fulfil all the other conventional requirements of social existence. Yet at another level, they retain their loyalty to the dead. The world of the dead person is the place they inhabit at a deeper, more authentic level. And hence there is always the danger that they may decide to join them literally, through suicide.

The feeling that others are simulacra is a phenomenon which is not found only in melancholia, although its presence in other clinical categories may derive from the same processes. At one level, if the melancholic lives with the dead, so the living will become just shadows. Lacanian psychoanalysis has a complex explanation of this, but for the time being let's propose a simple idea. What we find so frequently in such cases is a childhood marked by moments of *exchange*: quite early on, the child is passed from one parent to another after a separation, a step-parent replaces a parent, or some kind of loss takes place followed by an exchange of caregiver. This can also occur when there has been no real change in the identity of the caregivers, but if, for example, the mother is highly inconsistent with her child or if her way of being is suddenly altered by illness or accident. The key factor is a sudden change of state in those closest to us.

Confronted with a caregiver who changes from one moment to the next, or who is literally substituted for another in a dramatic changing of hands, what sense can the infant make of this? One solution, perhaps, to these terrible circumstances would be to imagine that the caregiver is actually more than one person, or an unreal one. It isn't that the same person has two different aspects, but rather that they become two different people. In one case, a woman described the decisive moment in her childhood when she knew that her mother was no longer her mother. When she was three and a half, the mother had arrived back from the hospital with a new baby, and she had the conviction 'This was not my mother, it was a different person.' From that moment, she felt that she was dead. 'Everything was over and gone. I had lost everything.'

This is reminiscent of Klein's observations on splitting in infancy. She believed that early life is characterized by the idea that different polarities – such as good and bad, satisfying and frustrating – are experienced by the infant as completely separate. They are attributes of different entities and not the same one: a frustrating and a gratifying breast or a good and a bad mother. Later, as the infant moves through what she calls the depressive position, he or she will realize that they are in fact attributes of one and the same entity.

In those cases where there has been a sudden changing of hands, the child experiences a dramatic removal of its fundamental points of reference. The person or people who mattered are just no longer there. While there are obviously a variety of ways of responding to such a situation, for some children the loss of such reference points is felt at a profound, symbolic level, altering the whole of their reality.

It isn't just felt as if one person is no longer there, but since this person was like a lynchpin in their environment, everything collapses. There is no longer anything to guarantee their reality, and so reality itself is suddenly revealed in all its precariousness. Nothing seems real any more.

Let's take another clinical example. B was brought up by his mother in a boarding house run by the Cs, a couple who showed love and affection towards him. His mother, on the contrary, could never hide her hostility to him and would berate him endlessly for the very fact of existing. When B was five, Mr C died, and within a matter of weeks the mother took him off quite suddenly to live with his biological father, whose wife had recently died. This moment was catastrophic for B. He was suddenly cut off from everything that mattered to him, not only through Mr C's death but through the isolation from the tenderness and care of Mrs C. Later, he would describe the trip to his new home as a kidnap: 'When I was kidnapped, I had to hold on to a place in another place.' In effect, part of B never left the home of the Cs.

No explanation for the move was given, and B was utterly bewildered when he was introduced to a man he was now supposed to call 'father'. From this point on, B said, he became uncertain about the meaning of words: 'What does the word "father" mean?', he would ask, just as he would speculate time and time again about his own proper name and even the personal pronoun 'I'. It was as if the uprooting had literally torn him not just from the care of the Cs but from language itself. Thereafter he became, as he put it, 'an addict of dictionaries', searching to pin down the meaning of words. These were not fanciful intellectual games for B but real, nightmarish preoccupations. How, he asked, could words have the same meaning before and after that night of the move away from the Cs?

From that point on, he was also alienated from his body image. 'All those years after Mr C's death, I walked around, talked, did my job, but I wasn't there. I was two people.' One day, B visited a museum and came across a medieval icon. It fascinated him, and, over many years, he would return to gaze at it. He yearned to break the glass that separated him from the icon, in order to 'access' it, to touch it somehow. In his analysis, B spent several years describing these visits, desperate to find the right words to describe the sense of his separation from the icon, the impossibility of reaching it and of saying what it was in the icon that he wanted to reach.

This impossibility matched precisely for B the impossibility of describing the deathbed scene of Mr C. 'It's like stretching out my hand,' he would say, 'to grasp something but there's nothing there.' Details of the scene would be run over again and again, accompanied by a terrible sense of the failure of words to 'touch' the scene itself. B knew that he inhabited both the world of the living and the world of the dead. But the true torment was the search to find words to describe this dual existence, this sense of being in two places at the same time. How could this impossible experience be communicated?

The icon, for B, was a symbol not simply of the dead man, but also of the impossibility of reaching him. If this man had been a crucial reference point for him, after his death he searched for 'a reference point for a reference point', a way of designating the compass that had so suddenly been torn away from him.

—

The sense of a gulf between social existence and utter solitude so carefully described by melancholic subjects can sometimes lead to a particular phenomenon. The person actually chooses to become quite literally anonymous, just one among others. As one woman put it, after giving up her high-powered career to take a far less stimulating nine-to-five job, 'I want to be a cog in a machine.' This quest for what she called 'banality' would allow her to disappear, as if to embrace the world of simulacra. This tendency had been noted by the psychiatrist Eugene Minkowski in the 1920s, and we might even see it as a version of suicide. If suicide in many cases is about making the choice of staying with the dead, thus cancelling out the duality of worlds, the quest for banality can be the inverse process. The subject chooses the world of the living, but living in the depleted sense described by this patient. Both suicide and banality imply a disappearance from life.

The reader versed in psychoanalysis might pause here, hearing an echo of a well-known saying about obsessional neurosis. This is assumed to revolve around the question 'Am I alive or dead?' Obsessives are thought to avoid any signs of life, in the sense of a proximity with the living, human dimension of desire, preferring to mortify themselves in mechanized routines of daily life which blot out any real encounter with alterity. Although a melancholia and an obsessional neurosis are as different as chalk and cheese, is there anything in this apparent juxtaposition of life and death? The melancholic, after all, may be both alive and dead.

Obsessives are very different from melancholics in that, first of all, their lives turn around questions rather than certainties. They worry and procrastinate without ever coming to any conclusion. They are often fascinated with the moment of transition between life and death. Bishop Berkeley, for example, became obsessed with knowing what happened between life and death, and between sleep and waking. He even arranged for himself to be hanged, failing to give the signal for his release in time and falling unconscious to the floor beneath his mock gallows. This interest in the in-between is the subject of many obsessive rituals, which often revolve around thresholds such as doorways, entrances, exits and barriers.

When bereaved, obsessional neurotics may hold on to an object that was there at the time of learning of the death. If they receive the bad news on the phone, they may fix on some item in the room, like a photo, a paperweight or piece of stationery. They may then make sure this object is close to hand while at the same time shunning it, keeping it in a drawer and avoiding touching it. They orchestrate a kind of private avoidance. The psychiatrist Vamik Volkan, who has studied these strange rituals, calls such prohibited items 'linking objects'. As links to the dead, they become the subject of all the procrastinations and rituals of the obsessive. They must be held on to yet avoided at all costs.

Such processes, however, have little in common with the all-encompassing identification with the dead we find in melancholia. It is also the reason suicide is so rare in obsessives. The pull of the dead is not so strong and the nature of the identification with the dead is different. They may hate the lost loved one, but they are less likely to internalize this so as to hate themselves. Obsessives, in fact, quite like themselves, which is why they may be most irritating to other people. They will gravitate towards and away from thoughts of death, which may in turn often disguise fears of bodily injury or mutilation. Likewise, it is rare to find extended states of depression in obsessional neurotics. It is nearly always a positive sign when an obsessional neurotic in analysis becomes depressed, as it indicates that the usual system of defences is no longer working and hence that change is possible.

—

The split between the 'unreal' world of social being and 'real' existence is rarely experienced without anguish in melancholia. The 'real' world inhabited by the melancholic involves such terrifying motifs as endless purgatory, minutes that last centuries, un-utterable pain and angst, and the call of the dead. These descriptions change historically, showing a basic feature of how our minds work. It is well known that a paranoiac person living in the 1950s may have felt persecuted by KGB agents, while today the persecutor might be an agent of the Opus Dei, popularized by the bestselling novel *The Da Vinci Code*. As each historical epoch privileges the representation of certain enemies

– witches, vampires, Nazis, KGB agents, aliens – these become equated with persecutors. They provide a way for the paranoiac person to identify their persecution, to give it a name. Cultural ideas are used to express the feeling of persecution, and these will naturally change over time.

We find the same process in melancholia. The idea of inhabiting two worlds will often be influenced by where a culture imagines the dead to reside – in the writer Derek Raymond's phrase, 'How the dead live'. The descriptions of heaven, hell or purgatory can then have a formative impact on the actual experience of the melancholic. They not only allow the melancholic to think, but they also provide the matter for their actual experience, as we saw with the feeling of time in the first clinical case we discussed. Once the doctrine of purgatory had been established from the thirteenth century onward, we find reports of melancholy subjects who thought that they had already arrived in hell. The historian Jacques Le Goff made the important point that purgatory was more a time than a place. People could establish calculations of time in purgatory based on the magnitude of their sufferings, to give a kind of 'accountancy of the hereafter'.

Le Goff describes the many efforts to establish a proportionality between earthly time and time in purgatory, a proportionality that related two quantities unequal in magnitude and different in kind. With this growth in the 'psychologizing of duration', the classic accounts of melancholia began to appear. Hell may have been of limited duration according to most theories, but a day there could seem as long as a year, and this is exactly what we hear from melancholic subjects. The resonance of languages is quite striking.

Interestingly, Le Goff's careful reconstruction of medieval ideas about purgatory bears the mark of his own experience. Invited by the historian Pierre Nora to give an account of his choice of profession, Le Goff described his mother's fascination with the Catholic imagery of suffering, renunciation and hell. He links his mother's 'masochistic devotion' to these images with her own mother's early death, and this spectre of maternal absence was to haunt his own life. After his birth in 1924, Le Goff's mother developed puerperal fever and hovered, in his words, 'for three months between life and death'. This terrible limbo would form exactly the subject matter of his later research: the strange margin between life and death.

As religious language provided a framework for melancholic despair, so one of the motifs of the care of souls in the sixteenth and seventeenth centuries was to distinguish between true sinfulness and the delusions of sinfulness which used religious doctrine to express themselves. As one contemporary physician put it, 'There are melancholics greatly tormented by the anxieties of a heavy conscience who, attaching great significance to trifles, imagine guilt where none exists. Distrusting divine mercy and believing themselves condemned to hell, they lament incessantly day and night.' These melancholic torments were fuelled, indeed, by religious debates which scrutinized the meaning of eternal pain: what sense, for example, did the word 'everlasting' have in Matthew's phrase 'everlasting fire and punishment'?

When melancholia became the subject of psychiatric debate in late nineteenth-century France, case reports contain again and again references to these periods of everlasting pain, yet combined now with a curious new detail. To take one example, Madame N——, a forty-five-year-old woman seen by the psychiatrist Jules Séglas, experienced a number of symptoms after the death of her child from meningitis. At first, she had feelings of weakness, malaise and general uneasiness. These quite vague symptoms then became more precise self-reproaches: she was the cause of her child's death. This conviction, which situated her in the position of a cause, brought with it a terrible sense of sin, which was in turn rationalized. The sense of sin, she thought, was due to her failure to have carried out her first communion properly. These ideas then become generalized: she had burnt her children by her crimes, she had killed everyone around her. As a punishment, her sins would last for ever: 'One day', she said, 'will last thousands of years.' Her negations then extended to her organs: she had no heart or lungs. She was immortal, but 'such an existence is impossible'. She was condemned, she said, 'to the impossible', guilty of the ruin of the universe.

Many of these motifs – such as the self-reproach and the sense of impossibility – are common in melancholia, but why the particular detail about a problem at her first communion? As we read through other case reports from this time, the same detail crops up again and again. There is always a problem at first communion. Although it could be seen as an artefact of the psychiatrist's interest, doesn't it indicate a way of designating a problem at the level of one's registration in the socio-symbolic world? Something has gone wrong at the moment the person must take up a new symbolic position, at the moment they undergo a symbolic rite of passage. And can't this symbolic impasse give us a clue to the melancholic's dilemma?

———

We saw earlier how the fourth element of mourning involved being able to give up what we were for the one we've lost. This requires reconstituting what we were for them, a difficult and painful process of self-exploration. It means uncovering the unconscious assumptions we have made about how others see us. We take on an image for others, after all, once we have decided how we think they see us and what it is they want. Often this work of reconstruction is blocked in melancholia. One subject spoke of all the moments in his life when he had been addressed, complimented, commended. But he never had the sense that he knew who they were complimenting. 'Who are they really talking about?' he would ask. He would recall endlessly different images of himself, as if they all offered possibilities to say who he was, yet none of them provided the definitive answer. 'Every time someone says to me "You are . . ."', he said, 'it implies a reference to someone else, but suppose there's no such reference?'

Isn't this evocative of the symbolic impasse evoked by Madame N—? Just as the first communion went wrong, so the entry into the symbolic world where one's position is fixed in the symbolic network is barred. Each time it is necessary to take on a symbolic position, there is only a void. This is exactly the melancholic's problem: the symbolic Other is not there to situate him, and so all he is left with is his own image, unanchored and unchained, left at the mercy of not the symbolic but the very real Other. With no stable anchoring point, no fixity in the way he situates himself in relation to the Other, how can any ideal point be established from which the person can see themselves as lovable? And so, perhaps, comes the certainty of being worthless, unwanted or condemned. And, perhaps, the very identification with the dead which we have seen to be at the heart of melancholia.

The choice of dying with the dead takes on a new sense here. The dead cannot be relinquished because without them one would be left at the mercy of something even more terrible. If the lost person provided a reference point and a barrier against an unpredictable and invasive familial environment, they must be preserved despite their empirical absence. Melancholia could thus be seen as a defence against the state of being a pure object open to every attack of an unloving and hostile world. If part of the fury at the dead is due to the fact that they have not just left us but, as the case of B shows so clearly, left us with someone else, then they cannot be relinquished without paying a terrible price. If we defined paranoia rather loosely as the state of being at the mercy of the Other with no available mediation, then melancholia could perhaps be seen, in some cases, as a defence against paranoia.

After the death of his foster-father and the departure from the family home, B would return there on Saturdays to see the beloved man's wife and her children. Going back, he said, 'was a search for the point from which I could be known'. The tragic loss had plunged him into a world 'in which I had to be someone else, and still somehow hold on to the other world in which I was B for others'. With the removal of his most basic system of co-ordinates, there was no Other to provide him with his identity. Later on, he would appeal to a string of women to find out, as he put it, 'who he was'. But he would always be loved by them 'as someone else, a little boy who wasn't real'.

⸺

The symbolic impasse poses special problems for the melancholic. A melancholic subject is in two places at once, two entirely different spaces that cannot be superimposed. But how can this agony be communicated? One of the features of melancholia noted over the centuries has been its association with artistic creation and writing. Indeed, in some historical periods, discussions of melancholia have emphasized this creative aspect far more than its depressive elements.

The melancholic has a particular dilemma. He is desperate to articulate his state, yet how can he describe where he is if he inhabits two places at once? From which place should he speak? The feeling of impossibility this generates is a common feature of melancholia. Historical case reports of melancholics and contemporary clinical practice illustrate this time and time again. There is always a reference to some form of impossibility, something the person must do, some task that cannot be done. This is very different from the clinical pictures of, say, many cases of paranoia or schizophrenia. Here, the person may indeed be in great pain and experience innumerable obstacles, but the emphasis won't be on the experience of impossibility itself. Paranoiacs, in fact, often have high hopes for the future.

Yet melancholics tell us again and again how their situation contains an impossibility. The clarity with which they can delimit this is quite remarkable. Crucially, this sense of impasse is *communicated*. This means that part of the melancholic's struggle is to do with language, with finding a way to express the impossible. It isn't that the melancholic has got a problem and then wants to express it, but that wanting to express – or feeling that expression is blocked – is actually a part of the problem. A melancholic is less likely to keep this to himself, as if there is a link between the feeling of an impossibility and the necessity to convey this. The sheer repetition of these features might suggest that there is a structural problem here. And this, in fact, is exactly what we find in Freud's argument.

When Freud differentiated mourning and melancholia, he argued that the focus on memories and expectations linked to the lost object will involve the relations between different systems in our minds. Thinking, he believed, involves at least two psychical systems, one linked to the perception of things and one linked to words and speech. He called these different levels the systems of word and thing representations. Thing representations consist of collections of memories and traces derived from these, while word representations are made up of the acoustic and semantic aspects of language that become linked to the thing representations. Usually, the two systems are tightly bound together. Freud suggests that mourning can be carried out because of the possibility of a movement between thing representations and word representations. This is facilitated by the preconscious system of the psyche which binds the two systems together and which enables a passage from one network to the other. As each aspect of the thing representation is made subject to the judgements of mourning, so the feelings linked to it are fractioned in what Freud calls a 'detail work'. They move from the thing representation to the acoustic image of the word and then to speech itself. The fact that the object must be accessed in all its different registrations in these systems implies that mourning will be a long and painful process.

Freud thought that in melancholia a barrier prevents the usual passage between systems of representation. Unconscious thing representations cannot be accessed through word representations, as the path through word representations via the preconscious is blocked. The melancholic is left in the limbo of the impossible passage from one to the other. Thus, at the heart of melancholia is a problem to do with language. Words and things seem radically separated for the melancholic. Here, it seems, is Freud's way of trying to articulate the symbolic impasse we have found in the descriptions of their situation given by so many melancholics. Whether we agree with Freud's theoretical framework of word and thing representations or not, it is significant that the difficulty he ascribes to the melancholic concerns language and systems of registration.

This not only opens up the interesting question of whether speech is necessary for mourning, but also brings us to a sense of melancholic self-reproach quite distinct from those we have discussed. A melancholic subject can, in some cases, continue their litany of self-denigration, in the very precise sense of being unworthy of doing some duty which, as we explore it, is linked to a duty of speaking properly about the lost love object and their relation to it. A melancholic can reproach himself endlessly for not being able to tell you with exactitude about something, not being able to reach something, just as B would chastise himself for his failure to describe the scene of his encounter with Mr C's dead body or the museum icon.

The problem here is the basic impossibility of making words touch their referent. Daniel Defoe saw this brilliantly when he proposed the Cogitator machine in his 1705 satire 'The Consolidator', designed to prevent melancholy by linking the mind directly to the object of thought. He hit the nail on the head here: that a central problem of melancholia is the reference of words to things. 'Preserving the Thought in right Lines to direct Objects', he proposed, would banish the 'Melancholy-Madness'. The melancholic suffers from the abyss separating language and its referents.

What does this imply clinically? If melancholia means that the passage from things to words is blocked, would the aim be to reverse this? Or, taking the idea of impossibility seriously, to try less to access so-called thing representations than to allow the person to find words to index the impossibility of the passage from thing to word representations, from one representational system to the other: *to find words to say how words fail.* And isn't that one of the functions of poetry?

Let's return here to the case of B. One day he spoke about a science class he had taken in school. They had compared the image of a stick with that of the same stick immersed in water. This intrigued him. 'How could two different things be the same thing?' he asked. How could something that was dead and inert in one image seem alive and almost animate in another? B linked this question with that of his own identity and the use of his own proper name. Rather than making the obvious link to the dead Mr C, it was his own self that the question related to, as if, in Freud's expression, 'the shadow of the object' had fallen on the ego. And as he reflected on these questions, B began to write poetry. His verses were concerned with dual states, just like that of the stick in and out of water. They would be about rest and motion or different dimensions of sound, but never about one single static state. Rather, they focused on the impossible relation between two apparently contradictory realities.

B was finding a poetic way to designate the impossibility of making two states coincide, the impossibility of his own position inhabiting two worlds. And, as he reiterated again and again, the impasse here was at the level of language, of words. How could words express his position? How could they name the impossible? What was the truth?

—

Poetry may be one pathway here, but the melancholic impasse may also generate violent actions which aim to do exactly what Defoe's machine had promised. Since words tend not to touch their referent, making them do so may involve violence – and this was interpreted by many post-Freudian authors exclusively as oral sadism and hate. To put it another way, the melancholic subject reproaches himself for failing to make the two worlds coincide, to generate an unbearable sense of impossibility which is distinct from the pain of mourning. In mourning, the sequential work of moving through one's memories and hopes linked to the lost loved one allows, as it were, a gradual fractioning off of agony and longing. In melancholia, the possibility of this process is compromised by the fact that the melancholic does not occupy a place from which such work could be started.

This variety of self-reproach is certainly not the only one to be found in melancholia, but we find it in enough cases to suggest that it warrants attention. In his fine study of melancholia, the psychoanalyst Frédéric Pellion has studied carefully the linguistic situation of the melancholic. And a sensitivity to this relation to language can be significant for clarifying the place of violent or self-destructive actions, which may on occasion be triggered when the clinician puts undue emphasis on one or the other of the melancholic's 'worlds'. Sudden, violent actions may occur here to demonstrate to the clinician what is the real issue. They can also be a form of appeal to a witness, someone to register what the person is going through.

From a clinical angle, a melancholia can certainly improve. But this won't be due to its transformation into a mourning. Clinicians who notice the link between the melancholic's condition and a loss are often tempted to try to make the person mourn. But this can be a dangerous aspiration. Mourning, as we have seen, involves a process of constituting the object. The mourner must constitute his object by separating the empty place of the fundamentally lost object from the images of the people who go into it. But the melancholic is faced with a difficulty here for the precise reason that there is no difference for him between the object and the place it occupies. It is as if a real empirical object like a person has come to embody the dimension of lack.

Rather than different people going into the place of a lack, one person has become completely identified with it. That's why losing them is the same as losing everything. This means that the loss of the loved person is experienced as an unbearable hole which threatens to engulf them at all times. The melancholic here is attached less to the one they have lost than to the loss itself. Lack now becomes a hole rather than a source of possibilities. The melancholic cannot separate from his object because the actual process of separating is ruled out. If mourning will be allowed by early internalization not of an object but of an object's absence, in melancholia the loss and the object are equated. And this can generate a wide variety of forms of trying to unstick oneself. Jumping into the hole is one of them.

We can have a sense of this melancholic transformation of an absence into something real and present in the work of a number of contemporary artists. Bruce Nauman famously produced a cast not of a table but of the empty space that the table bounded. Later, the British artist Rachel Whiteread made several casts of the empty interiors of architectural structures, the most celebrated of which is 'House', the huge concrete embodiment of the empty space inside a London house. And Cornelia Parker, with great elegance and wit, has made works from the silver swarf generated by the process of engraving words on to rings, from the 'lost acoustic' of instruments robbed of their sound and even from the eleven days once lost from the English Calendar. These very different artistic practices share a concern with giving absence a physical presence; they turn a negative space into something real and substantial. Whereas Nauman's and Parker's work does this with a certain lightness, Whiteread's monolithic structures might evoke for us the hole of melancholia; an emptiness that has become massive, unavoidable and omnipresent.

We saw earlier how the constitution of the object always involves a certain sacrifice. This could be evoked by the little bits of the body sometimes thrown into the grave in burial rites: a fingernail, a lock of hair, or even, in some instances, a finger. Mourning cannot continue until the person has given something up symbolically. In melancholia, however, there can be an attempt to separate from one's pain by a sacrifice that substitutes the whole of one's being for a fragment of the body. The melancholic becomes literally the object jettisoned in the grave. The sacrifice here is not of a part but of the person him- or herself. In a recent case, a woman attempted suicide by lying on a railway track. After the train severed her arm but did not kill her, she picked up the arm and went to throw herself off a bridge, as if the sacrifice had to be of *all* of her. Such suicides may be a desperate attempt to separate from the invasive thoughts and images of the lost loved one, just as they may also be attempts to join the dead or departed. The sacrifice in such cases is not symbolic but real.

The living here remain with the dead, as if the basic attachment cannot be relinquished. The severed arm might even be an illustration of this. Commentators were baffled by the woman's efforts to carry her arm with her, only to then jump off the bridge. Why, they asked, didn't she just leave the arm if she knew she was going to die anyway? Picking up the arm meant, they assumed, that she had chosen life and not death. But as well as indicating, as we noted above, that she might have aimed to sacrifice all of herself, doesn't it show, at another level, how perhaps she killed herself precisely because she couldn't bear to be separated from part of herself? Someone she loved, whom she considered unconsciously as a part of herself, had been lost and so she went to join them. The arm was another part of her image of herself, and so each loss – the person and the arm – was refused by her. She kept the arm, then, for the very same reason that she committed suicide.

—

We have seen how there is nothing simple about the ways in which human beings process the experience of loss. Even if our surface behaviour seems similar, our unconscious mental life shows a real diversity. Nearly all of the examples we have discussed presented what would be diagnosed as 'depression', yet the causes and mechanisms at play were never identical. Retaining a link with the one we have lost may be imperative, but how we do so will take quite different forms. Beyond so-called depressions we find a complex set of unconscious processes, which the concepts of mourning and melancholia allow us to study in the detail they require.

We must be careful, however, not to confuse these two structures. A difficult, protracted mourning is not the same thing as a melancholia. In mourning, we slowly detach ourselves from the dead. In melancholia, we attach ourselves to them. Clinically, the two are often poorly differentiated, and some further examples may help to make their boundaries clearer. A young girl is separated from her father when he leaves the mother, taking all the children with him except for her. A few years later, the mother decides to train professionally in another country, and so it is agreed that the girl will go to live with the father and her siblings. At the airport, the mother gives her a doll, and, in her new home, she holds the doll close to her every evening, creating quite consciously for herself a state of intense pain. The father and her siblings are unanimous in their harsh judgements and disparagements of the mother, yet the daughter feels an intense loyalty to her. She feels it is her duty to remember her mother, and she does this through the figure of the doll. This was what she called her 'commitment': 'I had to suffer', she said, 'so I could be with my mum.'

The condensed states of pain every evening were her way of remaining linked to the mother, of keeping her present rather than, perhaps, mourning her absence. This powerful link to someone who isn't there might remind us of the way that a melancholic's existence may be saturated with thoughts of their lost love. But it is in fact very different. Grown up many years later, the daughter would say that even when she was reunited with her mother, she still felt as if she, the mother, were absent. The real, empirical figure of the mother had not been enough to fill the hole of loss and absence in her life. We should separate here the general, constitutive lack that organizes most of our lives, and the real losses that may at times evoke it for us. In melancholia, there is no difference between these two dimensions.

In another case, a boy's mother died shortly after giving birth to him. The father would remarry soon afterwards and the only sign of the mother's existence was in the father's black moods: it was these, he said, and not any photos or mementoes, that bore witness to her life and showed that she had really existed. Later, this boy would remain caught in a cycle of moods that he could not give up, despite realizing how destructive they were for himself and those around him. It was as if giving up the moods would mean giving up his link to the only trace of the mother.

A similar attachment to traces of the dead can be found in a third example. A young woman suffered terribly in relation to her body image, tormenting herself endlessly for being too fat and for eating the wrong foods. Her father had died suddenly when she was a child, and his only real interest in her had taken the form of admonishments about her appearance and diet. Even as a young girl, he had criticized her with cruel comments that had reverberated in her mind ever since. During her analysis, she realized first of all that her attacks on herself for being too fat were direct derivatives of his attacks upon her. And secondly, that she had turned these external attacks into self-reproaches as a way of maintaining her link to him. The father's only legacy was a criticism of her body, and so by perpetuating it he would, in some sense, remain present.

In the first case, pain provides a bridge to an absent loved one. In the second, it is the presence of bad moods, and in the third the horror at her own image. Yet in none of the three cases did the bridge come to engulf the person, so that the loss of the loved one took over their whole existence. There was still a tension between the image of the person and the sense of lack, rather than an absolute equation between them. Another way to describe the difference here was voiced by a melancholic subject. He distinguished between the denial of a positive term and the affirmation of a negative one. Trying to find ways to speak about the father he had lost in his childhood, he contrasted the way that logic can put a negation sign next to a particular term (−(the man)) and how a negative term can itself be emphasized ((−the man)). In the first case, known as predicate negation, the sign of negation – or absence – is applied, as it were, externally to a term or concept (the man), whereas in the second, known as term negation, the negation is included within the term itself (the not-man).

This brilliant distinction is perhaps the very difference between mourning and melancholia, and is itself a topic in the philosophy of logic. Mourning involves the process of establishing the denial of a positive term, a recognition of absence and loss. We accept that a presence is no longer there. Melancholia, on the other hand, involves the affirmation of a negative term. The lost loved one becomes a hole, an ever-present void which the melancholic cannot give up his attachment to. Interestingly, in the philosophy of logic, it is not possible to translate the one into the other: predicate negation and term negation are fundamentally incompatible. And here again we find the impossibility we have noted so many times. Perhaps it is less logic than poetry that provides a way out here. As our lost colleague and friend Elizabeth Wright observed, melancholic subjects 'require the poetic to deliver them'.

Conclusion

A melancholic man once told me how he had contacted a certain writer, since he 'needed to find another kind of language'. When I asked him why, he said 'to talk about truth'. He continued to speak about a scene from a film he had seen decades previously, an American B-movie in which a hysterical woman sobs and wails while a detective tries to interview her. As she voices the grief and pain of the murder she has just witnessed, the detective barks at her 'Just gimme the facts.' It was this contrast between the truth of her loss and the facts demanded by the detective that so struck my patient. Truth, he said, is never the same as the 'facts'.

To take the example we mentioned earlier, when the mother of the boy who had confined himself in a suitcase after the death of his father was asked what he was doing, all she could see was the facts: her son was sitting inside a suitcase. What she couldn't see was the truth behind the facts: that he was sitting in a coffin. Circumscribing truth is never easy. What we find in so many cases of melancholia is how it necessitates creating a new language to talk about loss. This is a long and arduous process, and each person must find the form of language that suits them and their concerns best. This can never be predicted in advance.

To work with any depressive states means taking the distinction between truth and the facts seriously. Sadly, today it is the 'facts' that are deemed more important by most conventional forms of healthcare, which emphasize not the unconscious mental life of the sufferer but their observable behaviour. Reducing pain and getting rid of symptoms are deemed to be the central aims of treatment. Sleep, appetite and productivity must all be restored. Although this may of course be of the utmost importance, there is a danger here that a suppression of symptoms takes the place of an analysis of symptoms, which may recur, in altered form, later in life. The dimension of truth is stifled rather than elaborated.

We have seen the significance of unconscious processes in the mournings and melancholias that so often lie behind depressive states. To access and have an effect on these processes, we need speech and dialogue, and this is unlikely to be either short or sweet. In today's quick-fix society, treatments which claim to achieve rapid results will no doubt seem more attractive, especially to healthcare providers like NHS trusts and insurance companies. These treatments may improve our moods, making us less agitated and less reactive to external events, but they do not allow any real access to the source of our problems. Drugs can alleviate surface pain but they cannot affect personal, unconscious truth, which can only emerge through speaking.

The main alternative to drug treatments today is generally believed to be the use of the cognitive behavioural therapies. These tend to follow the medical model very closely, by assuming that specific problems can be targeted by specific treatments. Depression is seen as an isolated problem which must be targeted in the same way that a problem of physical health is often treated, regardless of its context and links to the rest of the body. Or, indeed, in the way that a missile attack on a terrorist installation is supposed to get rid of the problem posed by terrorism. The military hardware may impress us, capturing our childhood fascination with precision technology, but the problem is of course in no way eradicated. There is a confusion here between removing a symptom and its cause.

Promising specificity of intervention makes cognitive therapies popular with healthcare trusts, as it suggests that outcomes can be measured clearly, and cost-effective treatment can be monitored and pursued. But these therapies are based on an illusion. Patients are trained to realize that their depressed states are the result of cognitive errors and distortions in self-observation. Their symptoms stem from mistaken judgements about their situation. With proper cognitive processing, they will be able to see the world differently and close the gap between their ill-adapted behaviour and the behaviour that they – and their more mature therapist – aspire to.

Cognitive therapy was perhaps used most widely in the Cultural Revolution in China, where people were taught that depression was just wrong thinking. Separated from their families, unable to contact loved ones, subject to cruel punishments and witness to the murder or 'vanishing' of those closest to them, millions of people were 'taught' to devalue their reactions. The world should be thought about in a different way, and happiness and enthusiasm for collective causes should replace despair and despondency. Positive thinking should banish unhelpful and antisocial negative attitudes. This form of conditioning shares the aims of cognitive behavioural therapies today. The individual is taught to deny the legitimacy of their symptoms. Rather than seeing a symptom as the bearer of a subjective truth, as psychoanalysis does, it becomes a piece of faulty behaviour that needs to be corrected.

Let's take an example here of these two rather different worldviews. Vamik Volkan reports the case of an eighteen-year-old woman hospitalized for a serious anorexia. During her stay, the nurses noticed an odd pattern: whenever her weight went over ninety-nine pounds, she would refuse to eat or pretend to eat while in fact ingesting practically nothing. Following the resultant weight loss, she would then start to eat enthusiastically again and show no concern with her body image, until the next time that she weighed in at over ninety-nine pounds. Then the cycle of self-starvation followed by enthusiastic eating would continue once again.

Volkan was intrigued by the choice of the ninety-nine pounds, although none of those treating her had paid any attention to it. As they explored her past together, it became clear that she had become unwell three years previously at the time of her maternal grandfather's death. He had been an influential figure with a special closeness to his granddaughter. When he had been admitted to hospital with the illness that was to result in his death a few weeks later, he had weighed over 200 pounds. But when the grand-daughter saw his body in the coffin, he had wasted away shockingly. It was when she saw the dead body that she overheard a remark that the great man now weighed no more than ninety-nine pounds. At that moment, she fainted.

We can imagine how a well-meaning cognitive therapist might try to persuade the young woman that her behaviour was self-destructive. It repeated a fruitless cycle that benefited no one. She might be encouraged, then, to think about what the triggers were for the moments when she stopped eating. She would be advised to keep a diary of her behaviour and thoughts, to try to identify the patterns that required modification. And indeed, this attention from another human being and the work of keeping a diary might well have proven helpful. But they would have neglected the dimension of truth. Her symptoms expressed less a cognitive mistake than a subjective, personal truth, involving her identification with the devastated image of the grandfather. Where cognitive therapy might have tried to correct her behaviour, the analytic approach aimed, over the long term, to allow her to access her memories, thoughts and fantasies about the dead man and to see how these were linked to other unconscious aspects of her childhood and subsequent life.

This case brings out clearly the fundamental difference between truth and the 'facts'. We can imagine hospital staff worried about her ninety-nine pounds, assessing its possible risks in terms of a chart that set out the normal weight for a young woman of her age. But this attention to a norm would have neglected what the number ninety-nine meant for her, a detail which, as Volkan shows, only emerged through dialogue. It is surely important to recognize this at a time when speaking is progressively devalued in favour of a vision of human life in which destiny is reduced to the parameters of biology. And speaking, unlike taking a drug, requires a listener – someone whom the depressed person can address. If communicating the impossible is so central to the melancholic's experience, there must be someone to receive the communication, to help them in their arduous task of finding a new way to speak about a hole.

Mourning, as we have seen, also requires other people, who may help the mourner symbolize and even access their own response to a loss. The dialogue of mournings that we discussed in Chapter 2 can mean the difference between the mourning process getting started and an inertial state in which life seems to have nothing to offer and nothing changes. In Keats's words, the mourner must seek 'a partner ... in sorrow's mysteries'. And this is where the arts become so essential to human societies. Works of art, after all, share something very simple: they have been *made*, and made usually out of an experience of loss or catastrophe. Our very exposure to this process can encourage us, in turn, to create, from keeping a journal to writing fiction or poetry or taking brush to canvas. Or simply to speak and think.

In his bleak essay *Civilization and its Discontents*, Freud examines the way that civilization has built into it sources of dissatisfaction and despair. Running through the different historical responses to these problems, from religion to government, he concludes that no form of social organization can ever banish human misery. Certain renunciations are necessary for people to live together, and these will force us to pay a price in other aspects of our lives. When Freud comes to discuss ways that life might yet be made more bearable, he quotes Frederick the Great's saying that each person must invent a way to save him- or herself. Perhaps surprisingly, he makes no mention of psychoanalysis here. Instead, Freud names not psycho-analysis but culture as the only possible panacea for the terrible demands that civilized life places upon us. In other words, he is saying that it is the arts that can save us.

We could think here not only of the bursts of creativity that may take place after a loss, or even the vast panorama of arts linking creation with death, from catacomb paintings to ornamental urns, sculpted figures of ancestors, sarcophagi and mummy cases, funerary sculptures, wallpaintings, and all manner of works of music, art and literature. In a sense, it is less the content of these works, less the manifest association with bereavement or separation that counts. Rather, it is the fact that they have been *made*, since making supposes that they have been created from an empty space, from an absence. Engaging with how others have made something can not only encourage us to choose the path of creation ourselves, but also allow us to access our own grief and to begin the work of mourning.

An empty space, however, can never be taken for

granted. As we have seen, perhaps the work of mourning needs to create one. Doing this means creating a frame for absence. In a series of works, Sophie Calle invited museum curators, guards and staff to describe their memory of an absent painting, missing either through theft or loan. They were encouraged to draw or write about it, and their recollections were then displayed where the work itself had once been housed within the museum space. Having created an artificial frame, she drew out this creative work from within it. Her subjects were creating from a lack, but there was never any question that what they made would replace the missing work. Like an art of fractions, these pieces not only marked an empty place but constituted something real and substantial in themselves. Could we ever expect more from the work of mourning?

Notes

Introduction

p. 4 Sigmund Freud, *Mourning and Melancholia* (1917), *Standard Edition*, vol. 14, pp. 237–58.

p. 4–5 For background to the concepts of mourning and melancholia, see Stanley Jackson, *Melancholia and Depression* (New Haven: Yale University Press, 1986); Jennifer Radden, 'Melancholy and Melancholia' in David Michael Levin (ed.), *Pathologies of the Modern Self* (New York: New York University Press, 1987), pp. 231–50; Jennifer Radden (ed.), *The Nature of Melancholy* (New York: Oxford University Press, 2000); Lawrence Babb, *Elizabethan Malady: A Study of Melancholia in English Literature from 1580 to 1642* (East Lansing: Michigan State University Press, 1951); Hubertus Tellenbach, *Melancholy* (1961) (Pittsburgh: Duquesne University Press, 1980); Raymond Klibansky, Erwin Panofsky and Fritz Saxl, *Saturn and Melancholia* (New York: Basic Books, 1964); Froma Walsh and Monica McGoldrick (eds.), *Living Beyond Loss*, 2nd edn. (New York: Norton, 2004); and Carole Delacroix and Gabrièle Rein, 'Bibliographie sur Mélancolie et Dépression', *Figures de Psychanalyse*, 4 (2001), pp. 125–33.

Chapter 1

p. 11 Different views of depression, see Arthur Kleinman and Byron Good, *Culture and Depression* (Berkeley: University of California Press, 1985); Spero Manson and Arthur Kleinman, 'DSM-IV, Culture and Mood Disorder: A Critical Reflection on Current Progress', *Transcultural Psychiatry*, 35 (1998), pp. 377–86; and Alice Bullard, 'From Vastation to Prozac Nation', *Transcultural Psychiatry*, 39 (2002), pp. 267–94.

p. 11–12 Different manifestations, see J. Takahashi and A. Marsella, 'Cross-Cultural Variations in the Phenomenological Experience of Depression', *Journal of Cross-Cultural Psychology*, 7 (1976), pp. 379–96.

p. 12–13 Serge André complicates this view in *Devenir Psychanalyste et le Rester* (Brussels: Editions Que, 2003), pp. 149–54. On new images of autonomy, see Nikolas Rose, *Governing the Soul*, 2nd edn. (London: Free Association Books, 1999).

p. 13 Historians, see David Healy, *The Anti-Depressant Era* (Cambridge, Mass.: Harvard University Press, 1997) and *The Creation of Psychopharmacology* (Cambridge, Mass.: Harvard University Press, 2002); S. Jadhav, 'The Cultural Construction of Western Depression', in V. Skultans and J. Cox (eds), *Anthropological Approaches to Psychological Medicine* (London: Jessica Kingsley, 2000); Alain Ehrenberg, *La Fatigue d'Être Soi: Dépression et Société* (Paris: Odile Jacob, 2000); and Nikolas Rose, 'Disorders without Borders? The Expanding Scope of Psychiatric Practice', *Biosocieties*, 1 (2006), pp. 465–84.

p. 14 Scepticism about claims, see Ilina Singh and Nikolas Rose, 'Neuro-forum: An Introduction', *Biosocieties*,

1 (2006), pp. 97–102; Giovanni Fava, 'Long-term Treatment with Antidepressant Drugs: The Spectacular Achievements of Propaganda', *Psychotherapy and Psychosomatics*, 71 (2002), pp. 127–32; David Healy, 'The Three Faces of the Antidepressants', *Journal of Nervous and Mental Diseases*, 187 (1999), pp.174–80, and 'The Assessment of Outcomes in Depression: Measures of Social Functioning', *Journal of Contemporary Psychopharmacology*, 11 (2000), pp. 295–301.

p. 15 Depression as protection, see David Healy, *Let Them Eat Prozac* (New York: New York University Press, 2004).

p. 15 Lima, see Laurence Kirmayer, 'Psychopharmacology in a Globalizing World: The Use of Antidepressants in Japan', *Transcultural Psychiatry*, 39 (2002), pp. 295–322.

p. 15–16 Effectiveness of anti-depressants, see Giovanni Fava and K. S. Kendler, 'Major Depressive Disorder', *Neuron*, 28 (2000), pp. 335–41; S. E. Byrne and A. J. Rothschild, 'Loss of Antidepressant Efficacy During Maintenance Therapy', *Journal of Clinical Psychiatry*, 59 (1998), pp. 279–88, Peter Breggin and David Cohen, *Your Drug May Be Your Problem* (New York: Da Capo Press, 1999); David Healy, *Let Them Eat Prozac*, op. cit, and any issue of the journal *Ethical Human Psychology and Psychiatry*.

p. 24 Melancholy and creativity, see Peter Toohey, 'Some Ancient Histories of Literary Melancholia', *Illinois Classical Studies*, 15 (1990), pp. 143–61.

p. 25 C. S Lewis, *A Grief Observed* (London: Faber & Faber, 1961).

p. 26 'Hallucination of lost loved one', see Paul Rosenblatt, Patricia Walsh and Douglas Jackson, *Grief and Mourning in Cross-Cultural Perspective* (New Haven: HRAF, 1976);

Bernard Schoenberg et al., 'Bereavement, its Psychosocial Aspects' (New York: Columbia University Press, 1975); and Ira Glick, Robert Weiss and Colin Murray Parkes, *The First Year of Bereavement* (New York: Wiley, 1974).

p. 27 Between one and two years, see George Pollock, 'Mourning and Adaptation', *International Journal of Psychoanalysis*, 42 (1961), pp. 341–61.

p. 28 Sigmund Freud, *The Interpretation of Dreams* (1899), *Standard Edition*, vol. 4, pp. 339ff.

p. 30 Gordon Livingstone, 'Journey', in DeWitt Henry, *Sorrow's Company: Writers on Loss and Grief* (Boston: Beacon Press, 2001), pp. 100–120.

p. 30–31 On Poe, see Maud Mannoni, *Amour, Haine, Séparation* (Paris: Denoel, 1993); and Lenore Terr, 'Childhood Trauma and the Creative Product – a Look at the Early Lives and Later Works of Poe, Wharton, Magritte, Hitchcock and Bergman', *Psychoanalytic Study of the Child*, 42 (1987), pp. 545–72.

p. 38 'Les Observations de Jules Séglas' (1892), in J. Cotard, M. Camuset and J. Séglas, 'Du Délire des Négations aux Idées d'Enormité' (Paris: L'Harmattan, 1997), pp. 169–224. See also J. Cotard, 'On Hypochondriacal Delusions in a Severe Form of Anxious Melancholia', *History of Psychiatry*, 10 (1999), pp. 269–78; and Jean-Paul Tachon, 'Cristallisation Autour des Idées de Négation: Naissance du Syndrome de Cotard', *Revue Internationale d'Histoire de Psychiatrie*, 3 (1985), pp. 49–54.

p. 40 Christian Guilleminault et al., 'Atypical Sexual Behaviour During Sleep', *Psychosomatic Medicine*, 64 (2002), pp. 328–36.

p. 41 Sigmund Freud, *Totem and Taboo* (1912–13), *Standard Edition*, vol. 13, p. 65.

p. 44 Joan Didion, *The Year of Magical Thinking* (London: Fourth Estate, 2005), pp. 160–61.

p. 45 Martha Wolfenstein, 'How is Mourning Possible?', *Psychoanalytic Study of the Child*, 21 (1966), pp. 93–123.

p. 48 Helene Deutsch, 'Absence of Grief', *Psychoanalytic Quarterly*, 6 (1937), pp. 12–23.

p. 50 Billie Whitelaw, . . . *Who He?* (London: Hodder & Stoughton, 1995), p. 114.

p. 50 Breuer, see Freud, *Studies on Hysteria* (1895), *Standard Edition*, vol. 2, pp. 33–4.

p. 51 Towel, see Vamik Volkan, *Linking Objects and Linking Phenomena* (New York: International Universities Press, 1981), p. 75.

p. 51 Edith Jacobson, 'Contribution to the Metapsychology of Psychotic Identification', *Journal of the American Psychoanalytic Association*, 2 (1954), pp. 239–62.

p. 52 Lenin, see George Pollock, 'Anniversary Reactions, Trauma and Mourning', *Psychoanalytic Quarterly*, 39 (1970), pp. 347–71.

p. 54 Pollock on destiny, 'On Time and Anniversaries', in Mark Kanzer (ed.), *The Unconscious Today* (New York: International Universities Press, 1971), pp. 233–57.

p. 54 Marie Bonaparte, 'L'Identification d'une Fille à sa Mère Morte', *Revue Française de Psychanalyse*, 2 (1928), pp. 541–65.

p. 55 Bertram Lewin, *The Psychoanalysis of Elation* (London: Hogarth, 1951).

p. 55 Sigmund Freud, *The Ego and the Id* (1923), *Standard Edition*, vol. 19, pp. 28–30.

p. 58 Survivors, see Natalie Zajde, *Enfants de Survivants* (Paris: Odile Jacob, 1995).

Chapter 2

p. 60 Karl Abraham, 'A Short Study of the Development of the Libido Viewed in the Light of Mental Disorders' (1924), in *Selected Papers on Psychoanalysis* (London: Maresfield Reprints, 1979), pp. 418–501; Melanie Klein, 'A Contribution to the Psychogenesis of Manic-Depressive States' (1935), in *Love, Guilt and Reparation* (London: Hogarth, 1975) and 'Mourning and its Relation to Manic-Depressive States' (1940), in ibid. See also J. O. Wisdom, 'Comparison and Development of the Psychoanalytical Theories of Melancholia', *International Journal of Psychoanalysis* (1962), pp. 113–32; and Bertram Lewin, *The Psychoanalysis of Elation* op. cit.

p. 62 Jack Goody, *Death, Property and the Ancestors* (London: Tavistock, 1962).

p. 62 Eating, see Walter Burkert, *Homo Necans: The Anthropology of Ancient Greek Sacrificial Ritual and Myth* (Berkeley/Los Angeles: University of California Press, 1983).

p. 62–3 Otto Fenichel, 'Respiratory Introjection' (1931), in *The Collected Papers of Otto Fenichel*, vol. 1 (New York: Norton, 1953), pp. 221–40.

p. 63 Colette Soler, *What Lacan Said about Women* (New York: The Other Press, 2006).

p. 64 Sigmund Freud and Karl Abraham, *The Complete Correspondence of Sigmund Freud and Karl Abraham 1907–1925*, ed. Ernst Falzeder (London: Karnac, 2002).

p. 67 Robert Lifton, *Death in Life: The Survivors of Hiroshima* (London: Weidenfeld & Nicolson, 1968).

p. 67–8 For a critique of Klein, see Darian Leader, *Freud's*

Footnotes (London: Faber & Faber, 2000), pp. 49–87 and 189–236.

p. 69 Cheryl Strayed, 'Heroin/e', in DeWitt Henry, *Sorrow's Company: Writers on Loss and Grief* (Boston: Beacon Press, 2001), pp. 140–53.

p. 72 Emile Durkheim, *Elementary Forms of Religious Life* (1912) (Oxford: Oxford University Press, 2001).

p. 72 Geoffrey Gorer, *Death, Grief and Mourning* (New York: Doubleday, 1965).

p. 72 Luc Capdevila and Danièle Voldman, *Nos Morts: les sociétés occidentales face aux tués de la guerre* (Payot: Paris, 2002).

p. 73 'Set mourning back', see H. S. Schiff, *The Bereaved Parent* (New York: Crown, 1977).

p. 73–4 AIDS, see Gad Kilonzo and Nora Hogan, 'Traditional African Mourning Practices are Abridged in Response to AIDS Epidemic: Implications for Mental Health', *Transcultural Psychiatry*, 36 (1999), pp. 259–83.

p. 75 Klein, 'Mourning and its Relation to Manic-Depressive States', in *Love, Guilt and Reparation*, op. cit., p. 359.

p. 76 Mourning in Hellenistic culture, see Nicole Loraux, *Mothers in Mourning* (1990) (Ithaca: Cornell University Press, 1998); and Richard Seaford, *Reciprocity and Ritual* (Oxford: Clarendon Press, 1994).

p. 77 Mark Roseman, *The Past in Hiding* (London: Penguin, 2000) and 'Surviving Memory: Truth and Inaccuracy in Holocaust Testimony', *Journal of Holocaust Education*, 8 (1999), pp. 1–20.

p. 79 Martha Wolfenstein, 'How is Mourning Possible?', op. cit., pp. 93–123.

p. 81 Harvard research project, see Ira Glick, Robert Weiss and Colin Murray Parkes, *The First Year of Bereavement* (New York: Wiley, 1974).

p. 82 Winnicott and Lacan on hate, see Darian Leader, 'Sur l'Ambivalence Maternelle', *Savoirs et Clinique*, 1 (2002), pp. 43–9.

p. 83 Maud Mannoni, *Amour, Haine, Séparation* (Paris: Denoel, 1993).

p. 84 Philippe Ariès, *Western Attitudes toward Death from the Middle Ages to the Present* (Baltimore: Johns Hopkins University Press, 1974) and *L'Homme devant la Mort* (Paris: Seuil, 1977).

p. 84 Iran, see Byron Good, Mary-Jo DelVecchio Good and Robert Moradi, 'The Interpretation of Iranian Depressive Illness and Dysphoric Affect', in Arthur Kleinman and Byron Good, *Culture and Depression* (Berkeley: University of California Press, 1985), pp. 369–428.

p. 86 Hanna Segal, 'A Psychoanalytic Approach to Aesthetics' (1952), in *The Work of Hanna Segal* (London: Free Association Books, 1986), pp. 185–205.

p. 88 Ginette Raimbault, *'Qui ne Voit que la Grâce . . .', Entretiens avec Anna Feissel-Leibovici* (Paris: Payot, 2005), p. 192.

p. 88 Sophie Calle, *Exquisite Pain* (London: Thames & Hudson, 2004).

p. 90 Hysterical identification, see Freud, *Group Psychology and the Analysis of the Ego* (1921), *Standard Edition*, vol. 18, pp. 107–8.

p. 92 Vincent Sheean, *Lead Kindly Light* (London: Cassell, 1950).

p. 93 Freud, *Studies on Hysteria* (1895), *Standard Edition*, vol. 2, pp. 162–3.

p. 94–5 On Gogol, see Pollock, 'Anniversary Reactions, Trauma and Mourning', *Psychoanalytic Quarterly*, 39 (1970), pp. 347–71. On Van Gogh, Humberto Nagera, *Vincent Van Gogh – A Psychological Study* (London: George Allen & Unwin, 1967).

p. 96 Billie Whitelaw, . . . *Who He?*, op. cit., pp. 31–2.

p. 98 Margaret Little, *Transference Neurosis and Transference Psychosis: Towards Basic Unity* (London: Free Association Books, 1986), p. 301; and Helene Deutsch, 'Post-traumatic Amnesias and their Adaptive Function', in *Psychoanalysis: A General Psychology*, ed. Rudolph Loewenstein et al. (New York: International Universities Press, 1966), pp. 437–55.

p. 98 Ludwig Binswanger, *Sigmund Freud: Reminiscences of a Friendship* (New York: Grune & Stratton, 1957), p. 84.

p. 99 See E. F. Benson, *Queen Victoria* (London: Longman, 1935); Elizabeth Longford, *Victoria R.I.* (London: Weidenfeld, 1964); and Stanley Weintraub, *Victoria: Biography of a Queen* (London: Unwin, 1987).

p. 99 Milo Keynes, *Lydia Lopokova* (London: Weidenfeld & Nicolson, 1983).

Chapter 3

p. 102 Eighteenth-century humorists, see Larry Shiner, *The Invention of Art* (Chicago: University of Chicago Press, 2001).

p. 102 Boris Uspensky, *A Poetics of Composition* (Berkeley/ Los Angeles: University of California Press, 1973).

p. 103 Franz Kaltenbeck, 'Ce que Joyce était pour Lacan', unpublished paper.

p. 104 Ella Sharpe, *Dream Analysis* (London: Hogarth Press, 1937), p. 187.

p. 106 Group's customs, Peter Metcalf and Richard Huntington, *Celebrations of Death*, 2nd edn., (Cambridge: Cambridge University Press, 1991); Paul Rosenblatt, Patricia Walsh and Douglas Jackson, *Grief and Mourning in Cross-Cultural Perspective* (New Haven: HRAF, 1976); and Jack Goody, *Death, Property and the Ancestors* (London: Tavistock, 1962).

p. 109 Childhood phobias, see J. Lacan, *Le Séminaire Livre IV: La Relation d'Objet* (1956–57), ed. J.-A. Miller (Paris: Seuil, 1994).

p. 109–10 Use of words, see Darian Leader, *Freud's Footnotes* op. cit., pp. 212–16.

p. 112 W. G. Sebald, 'Anti anti-depressant', Lawrence Kirmayer, 'Psychopharmacology in a Globalizing World', *Transcultural Psychiatry*, 39 (2002), pp. 295–322.

p. 114 Sigmund Freud and Ernest Jones, *The Complete Correspondence of Sigmund Freud and Ernest Jones 1908–1939*, ed. Andrew Paskauskas (Cambridge, Mass.: Harvard University Press, 1993), letter of 27/10/1928.

p. 115 White men as return of dead, see Effie Bendann, *Death Customs: An Analytical Study of Burial Rites* (New York: Knopf, 1930), p. 171.

p. 116 Robert Hertz, *Death and the Right Hand* (Glencoe: Free Press, 1960).

p. 116–7 Relocation of dead, see Louis-Vincent Thomas, *Rites de Mort* (Paris: Fayard, 1985) and 'Leçon pour l'Occident: Ritualité du Chagrin et du Deuil en Afrique Noire', in Tobie Nathan (ed.), *Rituels de Deuil, Travail du Deuil*, 3rd edn. (Paris: La Pensée Sauvage, 1995), pp. 17–65.

p. 117 Christian tradition, see Norman Burns, *Christian Mortalism from Tyndale to Milton* (Cambridge, Mass.: Harvard University Press, 1972) and D. P. Walker, *The Decline of Hell* (London: Routledge, 1964).

p. 118–9 Myths about non–Western beliefs, Louis-Vincent Thomas, *La Mort Africaine* (Paris: Payot, 1982) and *Rites de Mort*, op. cit. On filiation and continuity, see Patrick Baudry, 'Le Sens de la Ritualité Funéraire', in Marie-Frédérique Bacqué, *Mourir Aujourd'hui: Les Nouveaux Rites Funéraires* (Paris: Odile Jacob, 1997), pp. 225–44.

p. 119–20 Lisa Appignanesi, *Losing the Dead* (London: Chatto & Windus, 1999), p. 8.

p. 121 Bouphonia, see Walter Burkert, *Greek Religion* (Oxford: Blackwell, 1985), and *Homo Necans: The Anthropology of Ancient Greek Sacrificial Ritual and Myth* op. cit.

p. 123 Self-harm, see Effie Bendann, *Death Customs: An Analytical Study of Burial Rites*, op. cit.

p. 123 Kenya fieldwork, see Odile Journet-Diallo, 'Un Enfant qui ne Vient que pour Repartir', in Joel Clerget (ed.), *Bébé est Mort* (Paris: Eres, 2005), pp. 29–45.

p. 126–7 'No hope names', see Odile Journet-Diallo, 'Un Enfant qui ne Vient que pour Repartir', op. cit., and Paul Rosenblatt, Patricia Walsh and Douglas Jackson, *Grief and Mourning in Cross-Cultural Perspective*, op. cit.

p. 127 Jean-Claude Schmitt, *Ghosts in the Middle Ages* (1994) (Chicago: University of Chicago Press, 1998).

p. 128–9 Childhood mourning, see John Bowlby, 'Grief and Mourning in Infancy and Early Childhood', *Psychoanalytic Study of the Child*, 15 (1960), pp. 9–52; and 'Pathological Mourning and Childhood Mourning',

Journal of the American Psychoanalytic Association, 11 (1963), pp. 500–541.

p. 131 Constitution of object, see Lacan, 'Le Désir et son Interprétation', unpublished seminar, 1958–9, 18/3/59 and 22/4/59. See also Sidney Blatt, 'Levels of Object Constancy in Anaclitic and Introjective Depression', *Psychoanalytic Study of the Child*, 29 (1974), pp. 107–57.

p. 130 Jean Allouch, *Erotique du deuil au temps de la mort sèche* (Paris: EPEL, 1995).

p. 136 Martha Wolfenstein, 'How is Mourning Possible?' op. cit., pp. 93–123.

p. 139–40 See B. Schoenberg et al., *Anticipatory Grief* (New York: Columbia University Press, 1974).

p. 141 Bertrand Russell, see discussion in Laurence Horn, *A Natural History of Negation* (Chicago: University of Chicago Press, 1989).

p. 142 Freud, *On Transience* (1915), *Standard Edition*, vol. 14, pp. 305–7.

p. 143 'Sexual traces', see Louis-Vincent Thomas, 'Leçon Pour l'Occident: Ritualité du Chagrin et du Deuil en Afrique Noire', op. cit.

p. 145 'Who we were for them', see Lacan, *Le Séminaire Livre X: L'Angoisse* (1962–3), op. cit.

p. 147 Lowry, see Darian Leader, *Stealing the Mona Lisa: What Art Stops us from Seeing* (London: Faber & Faber, 2002), pp. 26–8.

p. 148 Joan Didion, *The Year of Magical Thinking* op. cit., p. 197; Gordon Livingstone, 'Journey', in DeWitt Henry, *Sorrow's Company: Writers on Loss and Grief* (Boston: Beacon Press, 2001), p. 106.

p. 149 Jewish culture, see Froma Walsh, 'Spirituality, Death and Loss', in Froma Walsh and Monica McGoldrick,

Living Beyond Loss, 2nd edn. (New York: Norton, 2004), pp. 182–210.

p. 150–51 Queen Victoria, Christopher Hibbert, *Queen Victoria in her Letters and Journals* (Stroud: Sutton Publishing, 2000), p. 177.

p. 151–3 See Sophie Calle, *M'as-tu Vue?* (Munich: Prestel, 2003).

p. 153 Fort-Da, see Freud, *Beyond the Pleasure Principle* (1920), *Standard Edition*, vol. 18, p. 15.

p. 162 'I was their lack', see Lacan, *Le Séminaire Livre X: L'Angoisse*, op. cit., p. 166.

p. 163 Catholicism, see the discussion in Rowan Williams, *Teresa of Avila* (London: Geoffrey Chapman, 1991).

p. 163–4 Richard Trexler, *Public Life in Renaissance Florence* (New York: Academic Press, 1980); Jean-Claude Schmitt, *Ghosts in the Middle Ages*, op. cit.

Chapter 4

p. 173 Loss of books, see Stanley Jackson, *Melancholia and Depression*, op. cit.

p. 175 Lacanian psychoanalysis, see Lacan, *Ecrits* (Paris: 1966), pp. 567–8 and the essays in Geneviève Morel, *Clinique du Suicide* (Paris: Eres, 2002).

p. 176 Different mother, see Edith Jacobson, *Depression* (New York: International Universities Press, 1971), p. 210.

p. 179 Minkowski, *Le Temps Vécu* (Neuchâtel: Delachaux et Niestlé, 1968).

p. 180 Vamik Volkan, 'The Linking Objects of Pathological Mourners', *Archives of General Psychiatry*, 27 (1972), pp. 215–21.

p. 182 Jacques Le Goff, *The Birth of Purgatory* (1981) (Chicago: University of Chicago Press, 1984).

p. 183 Pierre Nora (ed.), *Essais d'Ego-Histoire* (Paris: Gallimard, 1987).

p. 183 'Melancholics greatly tormented', Lawrence Babb, *Elizabethan Malady* (East Lansing: Michigan State University Press, 1951), p. 38.

p. 184 Séglas, in J. Cotard, M. Camuset and J. Séglas, *Du Délire des Négations aux Idées d'Enormité* (Paris: L'Harmattan, 1997).

p. 186 Strictly speaking, we are talking here about a paranoid position rather than paranoia as such. Paranoia is a defence against being at the mercy of the Other, with the delusion aiming to give meaning to the situation. It's the difference between 'I'm being attacked' and 'I'm being attacked *because of* a plot against me.'

p. 187–8 For examples of the sense of impossibility, see Hubertus Tellenbach, *Melancholy* (1961) (Pittsburgh: Duquesne University Press, 1980).

p. 188–9 Word and thing representations, see Freud, *Project for a Scientific Psychology* (1895), *Standard Edition*, vol. 1, pp. 361–2, and *The Unconscious* (1915), *Standard Edition*, vol. 14, pp. 166–215.

p. 192 Frédéric Pellion, *Mélancolie et Verité* (Paris: Presses Universitaires de France, 2000).

p. 193–4 On negative objects, see Darian Leader, 'The Double Life of Objects', in *Cornelia Parker, Perpetual Canon* (Stuttgart: Kerber Verlag, 2005), pp. 72–7.

p. 198–9 On two forms of negation, see Laurence Horn, *A Natural History of Negation* (Chicago: Chicago University Press, 1989).

p. 199 Elizabeth Wright, *Speaking Desires Can Be Dangerous* (Oxford: Polity, 1999).

Conclusion

p. 204–5 Ninety-nine pounds, see Vamik Volkan, *Linking Objects and Linking Phenomena* (New York: International Universities Press, 1981).

p. 206 John Keats, 'Ode on Melancholy'.

p. 206–7 Freud, *Civilization and its Discontents* (1929), *Standard Edition*, vol. 21, p. 83.

p. 208 Sophie Calle, 'Disparitions' and 'Fantômes' (Paris: Actes Sud, 2000).

Typeset by Rowland Phototypesetting Ltd.

9 781555 975425